Grill Thrills!

Recipes and Inspiration for Creative Grilling

SHADY OAK PRESS

Grill Thrills!

Recipes and Inspiration for Creative Grilling

Tom Carpenter, *Creative Director*

Jennifer Weaverling, *Production Editor*

Julie Cisler, *Senior Book Designer*

Bill Lindner Photography, *Commissioned Photography*

Abby Wyckoff, *Food Stylist*

Pegi Lee, Susan Telleen, *Assistant Food Stylists*

Rhonda Watkins, *Prop Stylist*

Special thanks to: Denise Bornhausen; Terry Casey; Janice Cauley; Kim Coleman at The Coleman Company, Wichita, Kansas; Patrick Durkin; Elizabeth Gunderson; Jeff Halverson at Lindner's Green House and Garden Center, St. Paul, Minnesota; Amanda Hankerson; Mike Hehner; Cindy Jurgensen; Bea Krinke; Jason Lund; Chris McArthur; Nancy Maurer; Sue Ann Muller at The Outdoor Cooking Store, White Bear Lake, Minnesota; Mary Jo Myers; Ruth Petran; Martha Zeimer.

ABOUT THE AUTHORS

Bruce

Bruce Weinstein and **Mark Scarbrough** are a food and travel writing team. Bruce, a former advertising creative director, got his culinary training at Johnson and Wales. Mark, a former academic, has written extensively on food and cooking for the past six years. Together and separately, they have authored eight cookbooks, including the "Ultimate" cookbooks series, which includes *The Ultimate Shrimp Book* and *The Ultimate Brownie Book*. Regular contributors to *Cooking Pleasures, Wine Spectator, Gourmet* and *Cooking Light*, they live in New York City but grill in Vermont.

Mark

On the cover: Pork Chops Stuffed with Grilled Apple Chutney, page 51
On page 1: Portobello Mushrooms with Herbs de Provence Rub, page 134

1 2 3 4 5 6 / 12 11 10 09 08 07
© 2003 North American Membership Group, Inc.
ISBN: 978-1-58159-317-4

Distributed by:
Sterling Publishing Co., Inc.
387 Park Avenue South
New York, NY 10016-8810

For information about custom editions, special sales, premium and corporate purchases, please contact Sterling Special Sales Department at 800-805-5489 or specialsales@sterlingpub.com.

SHADY OAK PRESS

12301 Whitewater Drive
Minnetonka, MN 55343

TABLE OF CONTENTS

INTRODUCTION

Sometime in May, the evenings start to turn long, although it's barely noticeable at first. Supper gets pushed off fifteen minutes, twenty — after a pick-up basketball game, after a long walk, after one more cribbage match on the deck. Somebody finally says, "Hey, what's for dinner?" In the refrigerator, there's some chicken, some vegetables, or maybe some ground beef. Nobody wants to heat up the kitchen. Why not fire up the grill?

A month later, the afternoons and evenings start to stretch out even more. Friends arrive on the weekends, pile out of their cars — family too. Your kids invite kids over you've never seen before. Soon the yard's full of people. Somebody runs to the store for sodas, drinks. What's next? Why not fire up the grill?

Or maybe a thaw set in early this year. It's January or February, but you're in a T-shirt and jeans. Your spouse says you're nuts. No, just hopeful. Why not fire up the grill?

Grilling has become North America's passion. Quick and easy, it's no-fuss cooking for a world in a rush. But it's also part of our shared national heritage, a heritage that has roots all over the world — shish kabobs from the Middle East, tandoori chicken from India, portobello burgers from your local vegetarian co-op. Grilling may be the one culinary technique that's truly pan-national. It's certainly the one we have embraced full-on.

So here in *Grill Thrills!* is a simple guide to everything about the grill. Call it a starter kit. Call it a refresher course, if you're not a novice.

First, there's a chapter on the basics: what you need to know to get started or hone your skills.

Then there are recipes galore: some, straightforward; some, flights of fantasy. Some have long roots — Italian or Greek, for example. Others are classics, what you'd expect to smell across the fence when your

neighbor fires up the grill some evening after work.

There are enough recipes to last you long into winter and out again, back to those halcyon days of summer, those long days when food is just a way — the best way — to bring friends together.

Let this book be your guide on an exciting and taste-filled journey to *Grill Thrills!*

Pork Chops Stuffed with Grilled Apple Chutney, page 51

GRILLING SECRETS

Anybody can be a pro at the grill. It's really only a matter of finding the right type of grill for your taste, then learning how to tend its fire. Over the past ten years, there has been an explosion of grilling paraphernalia — some helpful, some just gimmicky. Here we'll review the more useful tools of the trade, then give you some basic tips to make your next cookout a success. All in all, consider this chapter a handy encyclopedia for grilling success.

GRILLING VS. BARBECUING:
A CLARIFICATION OF TERMS

When your father went out back and threw the steaks on the grill, you probably said to your friends, "Wow, Dad's barbecuing tonight." Nice memory, no doubt — but it's inaccurate. Technically, he was grilling. So let's define some terms.

Grilling. This involves cooking over direct heat — usually high, sometimes medium, but never low. When you grill, you put food right over the fire. The flames roil up and sear the outside, sealing in the juices — thus, the hallmark of grilling: charred outside, moist inside. In this book, *Basic Grilled Chicken with a Sweet and Spicy Barbecue Sauce* (page 75) and *Martini-Marinated Venison Steaks* (page 104) are good examples of straightforward grilling, the first with a mopped sauce to keep the chicken moist; the second with a marinade to tenderize the meat before it hits the fire.

Barbecuing. In contrast to grilling, this is an indirect cooking method. Barbecuing is not done directly over heat, but rather to the side of low or medium heat, never high heat. (Some folks, particularly from the Kansas City or Tennessee schools, claim it's never done with any heat but low — others, from Texas and California, beg to differ.) In this book, *Texas Brisket with a Classic Texas Barbecue Sauce* (page 34) and *Pulled Pork* (page 66) are prime examples of barbecue. Both have sauces (the brisket's, homemade; the pork's, bottled) because given the long cooking time, barbecuing tends to dry the meat out. That said, the flavors are deeper and more intense than those produced by simple grilling.

Indirect cooking. Over high heat, this is a hybrid sport, a modern concoction thanks to more efficient grills. *Beef Ribs with a Plum Barbecue Sauce* (page 38) and *Curried Salmon Fillets* (page 116) are, thus, neither grilled nor barbecued in the technical sense of the words. Indirect cooking over high heat is best for fatty meats or oily fish fillets. This method also allows sauces to set quickly to a glaze, rather than burn.

Of course, complicating the matter is the word "grill," which has come to mean any type of backyard cooking device, as well as those grated cook tops now sold with high-end kitchen set-ups. To be accurate, "you barbecue or grill on a grill." In French, they may have a different word for every single thing — but this is English. We have to multitask.

THE TWO BASIC GRILLS

The two grill types are identified by the fire used. Here are the more esoteric pros and cons of gas versus charcoal, along with other basic questions to consider when purchasing either kind of grill.

Gas grills. These grills fuel the flames with propane, either from a tank or an underground line.

Charcoal grills. These grills use briquettes (or wood chips) and offer a radiant heat, usually far hotter than that of gas grills. Buy a gas grill for the convenience, a charcoal grill for the taste.

Is the grill sturdy? The legs shouldn't wobble, even if you knock into the unit. And the lid shouldn't rattle in its grooves or be easily knocked ajar.

Are the handles heat-resistant? You must use grilling gloves or hot pads to open a grill or pull it around the yard, but you still want insulated handles for safety's sake. At the very least, look for wooden handles screwed onto a durable core (although the wood, unless repeatedly treated, will dry out and crack after being exposed to high heat for prolonged periods).

Is the grill grate secure? It should sit securely on its guides or ledges. Handles are a nice feature, so the grate can be easily removed for preheating or cleaning.

Is the grill grate narrow-gauged? Nothing is more irritating than a grill grate with slats so widely spaced that smaller cuts of meat or vegetables slip into the fire. Also make sure the grate is heavy-duty. One warning: too many cross slats perpendicular to the main slats can stifle efficient heating.

EVALUATING GAS GRILLS

So now we're left with the age-old question — at least since the 1950s — of whether to buy a gas or charcoal grill. We're unlikely to solve this debate right here, but we can offer some pros and cons. After some of the cons, we offer simple solutions, if available. Here are some specific questions to ask about a gas grill:

Is there a regulation gas valve? Don't be shy about calling your state's food or agriculture department for specifics on what is required of tanks and valves. If you buy a used grill, replace the valves and gauges to bring them up to code.

Does it have electric ignition? You should never have to reach into a gas grill with a lit match. Your father might have done so — but you may also have noticed he didn't have eyebrows.

Does it have adequate temperature controls? At the very least, the controls should have high, medium and low settings. What's the point of a gas grill if you can't adjust the temperature with the flick of a knob?

Does it have separate heating ranks? At the very least, a gas grill should have two grilling ranks, sometimes called "heating zones" or burners: right and left, perhaps, or top and bottom. Some higher-end gas grills have three, four or even five zones. You want to be able to turn on only part of the grill, or turn one part on high and another on medium.

UNDERSTANDING GAS GRILLS

Examine these pros and cons to evaluate whether a gas grill is right for you.

PROS	CONS
Expense. A standard propane tank can give up to 20 hours of grilling time. Propane is relatively cheap — depending on your state's taxes, a fill-up will cost between $10 and $15.	**Expense.** Gas grills themselves are costly. And frankly, they can also be temperamental, depending on the gadgets you've selected. Simply put, there's more to break on a gas grill.
Taste. Over a gas flame, as the old advertisement goes, you taste the meat, not the fuel. Propane burns efficiently and cleanly.	**Taste.** Gas doesn't infuse food with that traditional "barbecued" taste. You can use wood chips, but these add smoke, not charcoal charring.
Fire. With an electric ignition, you just open the tank valve, turn the burners on and flick the switch.	**Safety.** Gas grills have some safety issues, particularly with their tanks. Briefly put, if there's a problem — a leak or blockage — they can explode. Always maintain a gas grill according to the manufacturer's instructions. If a gas grill doesn't start immediately, shut off the gas and wait 5 minutes before trying again. Do not stand over a grill pressing the ignition over and over again while the gas is flowing.
Indirect cooking. This method is much easier on a gas grill — you needn't build a fire around a drip pan or to one side of the grill. Simply turn on one rank (burner) and you're ready to barbecue over the "off" rank.	**Moisture.** When propane burns, the attendant chemical reaction releases water vapor. Some food-snobs claim meats and particularly vegetables grilled over gas come off the grate "soggy."
Cleanup. Just turn the grill off with a flick of a knob. Scrape the grate clean of any residue later.	**Smoking.** Wood chips can be placed on the lava rocks, but the chips make quite a mess as they burn. You'll be stuck scooping ashes out of your grill — that is, doing something you bought a gas grill to avoid. If your gas grill doesn't have a smoke box, place the chips in a heavy-duty pan, either a disposable aluminum roasting pan or a metal loaf pan set aside for this purpose.
	Gas tank. Place it in a box to carry it to the refilling station — never transport it on its side. Air must be removed, especially when a tank is new. Alert the service person who fills your tank if this is an issue.

EVALUATING CHARCOAL GRILLS

If you decide to go the charcoal route, here are some specific questions to consider about that type of grill:

Is the ember grate secure? Most charcoal grills have two grates: one for the food, another the coals (the ember grate). Make sure the lower, smaller ember grate is secure and level. It can spell disaster if hot coals slip out of the bottom air vents while you're grilling.

Are there proper vents? We recommend top and bottom vents — that is, both in the lid and under the ember grate. You must control the fire by controlling its oxygen supply (in other words, by opening and closing vents).

Is the grill itself large enough? Unless you choose a hibachi (page 13), buy a charcoal grill large enough to handle direct and indirect cooking. If you buy a small grill, you may not be able to barbecue — that is, cook over indirect heat — because the grill's surface area is not large enough to hold both an ember bed and a spot away from the heat for the food.

SAFETY CONCERNS FOR ALL GRILLS

Always follow these guidelines when grilling.

- Be alert, especially when children are present. Set some basic rules: No roughhousing around the grill. Never leave a lit grill unattended.
- Drink responsibly when you're grilling. In truth, you're working with an enormous, mobile, high-heat oven, one that rises to temperatures (sometimes over 700°F) most home ovens could not withstand.

UNDERSTANDING CHARCOAL GRILLS

Examine these pros and cons to evaluate whether a charcoal grill is right for you.

PROS	CONS
Taste. You always get that traditional "barbecued" taste. Furthermore, smoking is quite easy — simply throw soaked chips on the coals.	**Safety.** A charcoal grill, particularly the kettle-drum variety, can tip over. Buy a solidly constructed grill. It can also spew embers, especially out of its bottom vents. Never grill over dry leaves or dry grass.
Fire. Charcoal simply burns hotter than gas. Beef, game and some vegetables are generally better over a higher heat.	**Cleanup.** The coals must cool completely before they can be removed. It's usually the next day before you can get to it.
Expense. Charcoal grills are far cheaper than gas grills, with almost no mechanical parts to break.	**Expense.** While the grill itself is cheaper, its fuel is more expensive, considering how much charcoal you have to buy to come out to the 20 hours of grilling time a standard propane tank can afford.
Thrill. Let's face it — charcoal grilling is a hands-on experience. You have to fuss with the grill and the food as it cooks. The smells, the constant checking, the fire — it's just downright fun.	**Hot spots/Cold spots.** You'll move the food all over the grate before you're done with a meal. Charcoal grills can go hot or cold in spots surprisingly fast — thus, the constant checking familiar to anyone who's worked with them. And maintaining a constant temperature in a charcoal grill is always a chore. There's no way around this, although there are some techniques to building efficient fires (page 14).
Ambience. No matter how you slice it, a charcoal grill just looks and smells, well, like summer, or a good backyard party.	

GRILL ALTERNATIVES

There are two alternatives to gas or charcoal grills. These are especially good choices if you live in an apartment or other urban enclave. A **hibachi** is good only for grilling: that is, for direct, high-heat cooking. Use hibachis only in large, open, well-ventilated areas. A second urban alternative is the **electric grill,** which is also designed for grilling, not barbecuing.

THE POINT OF GRILLING: THE FIRE

What would grilling be without fire? Just cold meat. So you must light the fire, and then manage two factors: how hot it burns, and how the food is placed over it.

FIRE AND GAS GRILLS

Lighting the fire. Read the instruction booklet; follow the manufacturer's instructions. In most cases, open the lid, open the gas tank's valve, set the starter-burner or one heating rank to high, then press the ignition switch. If the grill fails to light within seconds, shut the whole system down: Turn off the starter-burner or the heating rank; close the valve and wait five minutes for the gas to air out.

Once it is lit, preheat a gas grill 10 minutes on high before adding food to the grate and turning the temperature controls to the desired heat. If you're using wood chips or herb sprigs to flavor the food, add them to the lava rocks as you preheat the grill; let them start to smoke before placing any food on the grill grate.

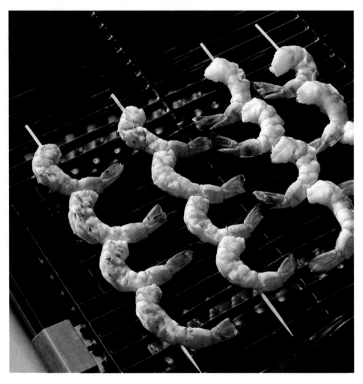

Maintaining the fire. As long as you've got enough fuel, maintaining the fire is just a matter of the temperature control knobs: set them as indicated by the recipe. If your gas tank doesn't have a gauge, you can find out how much gas you have before you begin grilling by tipping the tank to a 45-degree angle and pouring 1 cup boiling water all over it, being careful not to wet the valve or its casings. The section of the tank that remains cool to the touch still has fuel.

Cooking over direct heat. Simply place the food on the grate directly over the flame. You needn't light all the ranks or zones if you don't need to.

Cooking over indirect heat. Whether you know it or not, the ease of indirect cooking (barbecuing) is why you bought a gas grill. Begin by preheating one of the heating zones, either top or bottom, right or left, or some such configuration. Some grills have a heating zone with a more prodigious flame, specifically designed to be the one lit during indirect grilling — follow your manufacturer's instructions. Once the grill has preheated 10 minutes on high, place the food over the section of grill grate without a flame under it. Adjust the temperature control for the "heated" part of the grill as directed in the recipe.

Using wood chips on a gas grill. Place the soaked and drained wood chips in the smoker box, if available, or put them in a disposable aluminum pan or a metal loaf pan specifically set aside for this purpose. Place the pan directly on the lava rocks, or directly over one of the lit heating ranks.

FIRE AND CHARCOAL GRILLS

Lighting the fire. Fully open the bottom air vents, uncover the grill and remove the grill grate. Then proceed in one of three ways:

Liquid starter. Build a briquette pile on the ember grate. Create a conical pile at least 4 inches high and slightly larger than the food you want to grill. Don't be stingy: use a handful more briquettes than you think you'll need. Liquid starters always seems to leave a little "taste residue" on the food, no matter how long you let the fire burn.

Electric starter. This starter is odorless, tasteless and quite convenient. Build the briquette pile over the starter, which will automatically rake the coals into a bed as you pull it out of the pile. This requires an electrical outlet near the grill — and the best place for a hot charcoal grill is not against the house, under the eaves.

Charcoal chimney. These create the hottest, fastest fire by far. Stuff it on the bottom with newspapers, on the top with briquettes, as indicated by the instructions. Light it, then release the coals when they have ashed. Unfortunately, all this fandango is quite clumsy; always wear grilling gloves. No matter which method you use, it will take about 30 minutes before you're ready to cook. Let the coals become red, then rake them into a thick bed with a grill rake, or a small shovel or garden trowel set aside for this purpose. Once the coals are raked, place the grill grate back on its ledges or in its grooves, then give the coals about 10 minutes to become covered with a fine ash coating.

Maintaining the fire. Once the fire is going, adjust the air vents to regulate the temperature. You'll have to finesse the vents as the food cooks, to maintain the proper temperature. Larger charcoal grills often have vents both in the lid and under the ember grate. Those on the top are for smaller temperature gradations; those on the bottom, for major shifts. As a rule of thumb, open all the vents completely for high heat; close the bottom vents halfway for medium and to a crack for low, working only with the top vents for smaller gradations as the grill heats up or cools down.

If you're barbecuing for hours, you'll need to replenish the coals. Charcoal fires lose up to 150°F every hour they burn. To replenish the fire, add unlit coals to the grill — but increase the cooking time 10 minutes for every addition you make. Also leave the lid off for those 10 minutes, so the coals ignite with maximum oxygen concentration. Admittedly, it's a trick to lift off the grill grate while food's on it. You might want to purchase a grill clamp, designed for this task; it latches onto the grate to lift it off. Otherwise, use grill mitts to lift the grill grate by its handles. In either case, adding briquettes is probably a two-person job.

Cooking over direct heat. Simply place the meat on the grill grate, four to six inches directly over the coals; adjust the temperature with the vents.

Cooking over indirect heat. You'll need to maintain a fire to one side of the grill, or all around a drip pan set in the center of the ember grate. But don't build a briquette pile on the side when you start. Instead, build it in the middle of the ember rack as you normally would, then rake it to one side before you begin cooking. You can rake an opening for the drip pan, if you're setting it in the center of the ember rack. Or you can set the drip pan to one side of the ember rack, the coals on the other. If so, remember the coals are now against the grill's metal side. It will become super-heated, so be very careful working around it.

Using wood chips on a charcoal grill. Simply toss soaked and drained chips directly onto the coals once they have ashed over. Do not add so many that they put out the fire; if you're cooking for a long time, you can add more later. Or place the chips in a small, disposable aluminum pan or a metal loaf pan, then set this pan to the side of the embers.

CHARCOAL GRILLS: TEMPERATURE NOTES

Some charcoal grills now come with a temperature gauge just under the lid, or built into it. If yours doesn't, buy an oven thermometer that can hang off the grilling rack to the far side of the grill. Here is a handy reference to the heat levels in a charcoal grill:

- High Heat   500°F
- Medium Heat   375°F
- Low Heat   300°F

These temperature guidelines are not rocket science — mere approximations, at best. A charcoal grill, after all, is a low-tech gadget; it works by "feel" more than gauges.

Thus, it's no wonder experienced grillers test their grills by "feeling" the heat. If you want to do the same, place your open palm five inches above the grill grate. The fire is . . .

- High if you have to move your hand in 2 seconds.
- Medium if you have to move your hand in 5 seconds.
- Low if you have to move your hand in 10 seconds.

WHEN IT'S DONE, IT'S DONE

Grills can be finicky, and they're all different. So don't treat the timing in this book's recipes as a law brought down off the mountain by Moses. The times are guidelines, not rules. Use a meat thermometer for an exact measure of when something's done.

FEEL TEST

Experienced chefs can press a finger against a piece of meat and know how it's done by the resistance.

Rare. Meat will feel like the excess flesh in the curve between your index finger and thumb, if both are relaxed.

Medium-rare. Meat feels like the excess flesh just under your little finger, along the side of your hand.

Medium. Meat feels like the fleshy part of your hand between your thumb and index finger, about one inch down from where you tested for rare.

Well-done. Meat feels about like the center of your wrist.

DONENESS TEMPERATURES

According to USDA guidelines, these are the temperatures required of meat at varying doneness levels.

Beef and Lamb

Rare	140°F (not suggested for lamb)
Medium-Rare	145°F
Medium	160°F
Well-Done	170°F (ground beef must be cooked to a minimum of 170°F)

Pork

Rare/Medium-Rare	Not suggested
Medium	160°F
Well-Done	170°F

Chicken and Turkey

Rare/Medium-Rare	Not suggested
Medium	160°F
Well-Done	180°F

BEYOND THE GRILL: SOME TOOLS OF THE TRADE

In addition to a grill, you'll need a variety of other tools to make grilling safe, efficient and rewarding.

Butcher twine. This is invaluable for tying up roasts and whole fish, especially when they're stuffed. Butcher twine is usually available in supermarkets and gourmet stores. Don't substitute sewing thread or yarn — they may contain dyes and solvents not approved for human consumption.

Brushes and mops. Technically, a grill brush looks like a paintbrush; a mop, like a small kitchen mop. Aficionados claim brushes are better for thin sauces; mops, for thick sauces. Actually, they're just about interchangeable — except a brush is easier to clean and dry than a flop-headed mop.

Grill rake. This tool, specifically designed for a charcoal grill, rakes the coals into an even bed. Metal-handled rakes are sturdier, but can also burn your hands if you let them get too hot.

Metal spatulas and tongs. There's a long running debate between those who use tongs (now the fashionable set, if you watch the TV food programs) and those who use metal spatulas. Why choose? Spatulas are best for burgers, fruits and fish fillets; tongs, for heavier cuts of meat. Sometimes, as with a pork shoulder roast, you need both — tongs to steady, a spatula to support. In any event, buy long-handled utensils so you can pick up heavy items without getting your hands near the heat.

Drip pans. When barbecuing over indirect heat, drip pans are a cleanup time-saver, especially if you're cooking a fatty cut of meat or a "fatted" dish. Drip pans catch the excess fat that leaches off during the long, slow cooking. We recommend disposable, aluminum roasting pans, found in most supermarkets.

Fire extinguisher. In a real emergency, nothing takes the place of a fire extinguisher. Make sure you have one on hand whenever you grill.

Grilling gloves. These leather, suede or composite gloves help you get items off the grill without burning your hands. Depending on the type of glove, you can actually reach into the grill and take the meat off the grate without tongs or a spatula. Look for gloves that come up over your wrists. And check their "washability" — some need to be dry-cleaned, a fussy step in a griller's world.

Meat thermometers. A meat thermometer is best for determining when the meat is cooked to the proper temperature. Always insert the thermometer into the thickest part of the meat, so that it reaches the center of the meat, taking care to miss any bones or stuffing. (For a chart of USDA-approved temperatures, see page 18).

New inventions include instant-read thermometers, which tell the temperature the moment they're inserted into the meat; and instant-read meat thermometer forks, which you stick into the meat to take its temperature. The disadvantage to the fork is that you stab the meat twice, not once, for each temperature check you make, thereby letting twice as much valuable juice run out.

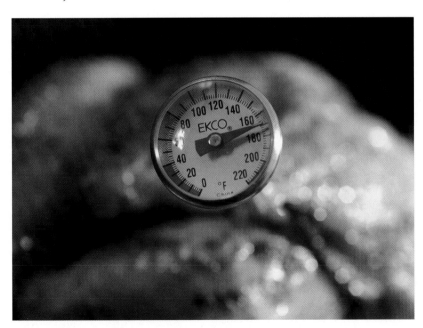

A digital remote thermometer may be the newest toy on the grilling market. You set the probe in the meat, then carry a beeper-like receiver with you. If you pre-set it to a selected temperature, the receiver will ding when your food is done.

Grilling baskets. Although no recipes in this book call for barbecue baskets per se, they are offered occasionally as alternatives. Baskets take the mess out of fish and vegetables on the grill. Fish fillets (and whole small fish like trout) can break apart; vegetables can be tedious to turn. A basket solves all this: flip it over with no fuss. The problem is the handle — it can stick outside the grill's lid, not allowing it to close properly. Recently, baskets with detachable handles have begun to show up in cookware sections. In any case, buy one thin enough to hold your food, but not so thin as to crush it when the lid closes.

Skewers. Metal or bamboo — that's the choice here. Either way we recommend long skewers, about 18 to 20 inches, or more, if you can find them. Metal skewers cook faster, since the metal heats the food from the inside. Bamboo skewers must be soaked in water 20 minutes before they're placed on the grill; otherwise, they catch on fire. Even so, their exposed ends still may flame up; wrap the ends in aluminum foil for protection.

Spray bottles. Sometimes there's one briquette so larded with fat, it won't quit flaming up. There's nothing better to put out that small fire than a spray bottle of water. A child's water pistol will work, too.

Carving board with trough. When you transfer food to a carving board with a built-in trough running along all four edges, the juices can't run onto the counter as you let the food rest, or as you carve it.

Grate brush. For cleaning up, use a stiff brush, preferably one with metal bristles (page 24).

Rotisserie. Some foods are wonderful cooked in the long, slow process that a rotisserie provides. Don't be fooled — it's not low-fat cooking. The meat's melted fat rolls around the whole cut, coating it in a crispy coating. It's best to use a drip pan under a rotisserie attachment. Most manufacturers make spits and rotisseries designed for their own grills. Unfortunately, a few are designed poorly: they're set up too high and the grill lid will not close completely when the rotisserie is engaged. Check first before making any purchase.

ROTISSERIE DONENESS CHART

Although the most accurate read is with a meat thermometer inserted into the thickest part of the meat, here are some helpful guidelines for foods cooked on a rotisserie over a drip pan at high heat:

1 (3- to 4-lb.) chicken	35 to 70 minutes
1 (5- to 6-lb.) duck	1½ to 2 hours
1 (3- to 3-½ lb.) pork loin	1½ to 2 hours
1 (5- to 6-lb.) rib roast	2 to 2½ hours
1 (6- to 7-lb.) turkey	3 to 4 hours

CLEANLINESS IS NEXT TO . . . GOOD GRILLING

There are some health concerns with food particles left on the grate for long periods of time, even if the food has been charred. Simply scrape a grill grate with a stiff-bristle brush — but not until it shines like new. The grate should still be blackened when you're done.

Don't use soap and water. Want to watch professional chefs cry? Take soap and water to their omelet pans. Professionals work for years to build up a nonstick coating on cast iron. You should strive for the same on your grate. Even after one or two uses, it has become "seasoned" — in other words, it's developed a natural nonstick finish thanks to oils, fats and sugars burned onto it.

Of course, the grate is not the only thing that gets dirty. Charcoal grills pile up with ashes, usually inside the grill well and perhaps in the ash pan, placed under the bottom air vents. To clean out the ash, always wait until the grill is completely cool, preferably the next day. A hot ember lost in the ash could set a trash bag ablaze. Never clean out the ashes with your hands; use a fireplace ash scoop, a small shovel or a garden trowel.

If you've used a disposable aluminum drip pan, let it sit in the grill overnight until the rendered fat hardens. If your grill has a permanent drip pan (sometimes called a "catch pan"), let the fat harden, usually for 24 hours. Scrape it out with a large spoon; dispose of it in a sturdy plastic bag or a disposable plastic container. Whether the fat is in a disposable drip pan or a plastic trash bag, seal your garbage cans tightly. Rendered fat is tempting to all sorts of animals, domesticated and wild.

GRILLING TECHNIQUES AND TIPS

Here's a potpourri of grilling insights that will help make the difference between just another meal on the grill … and a grilling sensation!

Don't forget your *misenplace*. It's a French term, essentially meaning "everything in its place." In cooking terms, it means you should get everything ready before you start cooking: get out the spices, quarter the onion, set out the tongs, you get the idea. When everything's at the ready, the recipe can flow through its steps — no awkward rummaging for basil while the scallops burn to a crisp on the grill.

Bring foods to room temperature before grilling them. Refrigerated meat takes longer to heat — sometimes so long that the outside burns before the inside cooks.

Oil the grill grate. With a charcoal grill, the grate is off while the coals are heating. Simply oil it with a paper towel coated in oil before placing it back on the grill. With a gas grill, it's trickier. Don't use paper towels, for they can ignite over the flames. It's best to use a brush specifically set aside for this purpose. Recently, oiling brushes have begun showing up in cookware stores. These brushes look like large kitchen sponges with heat-resistant, plastic handles. Under no circumstances should you ever use an aerosol spray oil, such as nonstick sprays, on a lit grill — it's an automatic blowtorch and a recipe for disaster.

Cover the grill. The lid should be closed while the food cooks, even if you're occasionally opening it to mop something with sauce. Resist the urge to check again and again — trust that the steaks haven't walked off the grate.

Forget the meat fork. When food is on the grill, the intense heat seals in the juices. So don't stick your food with a fork to turn or get it off the grate — that only lets the juices run into the fire where they do no one any good. Turn everything with a spatula or tongs.

Let the meat rest before serving. It's a hard moment: you're hungry, everything's hot, your guests have gathered around. Then the meat has to sit there on the carving board, doing nothing while you wait. But it's not doing nothing. The juices are setting up, the fat is stabilizing and the fibers are loosening again after they've clenched over the heat.

Carefully wash work surfaces and carving boards. Many of these recipes ask you to work with raw meat directly on a work surface, or let it rest on a carving board. Always clean these surfaces afterward with soap and very hot water.

Vietnamese Grilled Beef Salad, page 44

BEEF

Nothing sums up a passion for the grill like a strip steak or beef tenderloin, charred outside and juicy inside. Beef is very forgiving on the grill. It doesn't need to be brined, turned this way and that, or pampered. For most of these recipes, just cook it over direct, high heat — it's done in minutes. Beef is just about the perfect meat for grilling.

STRIP STEAKS WITH ROSEMARY HONEY BUTTER

Whether you call them New York or Kansas City strips, these are quintessential grill fare. They're simply the short loin minus the bone and tenderloin — in other words, the large sides of Porterhouse steaks.

MARINADE

- ½ cup olive oil
- ¼ cup chopped fresh rosemary
- 3 garlic cloves, crushed
- 1 teaspoon salt, preferably sea salt or kosher (coarse) salt
- 1 teaspoon freshly ground pepper
- 4 (12-oz.) strip steaks, trimmed

ROSEMARY HONEY BUTTER

- ¼ cup (½ stick) unsalted butter, barely softened
- 2 tablespoons finely chopped fresh rosemary
- 2 teaspoons cracked black peppercorns
- 2 teaspoons honey
- 1 teaspoon salt

1 **For Marinade:** In small bowl, combine olive oil, rosemary, garlic, salt and pepper; mix well. Place steaks in large baking dish. Top with marinade; turn to coat. Cover; refrigerate at least 4 hours, preferably overnight, but no more than 24 hours, turning occasionally.

2 Heat grill for direct cooking. Bring steaks and marinade to room temperature. (Depending on its viscosity, oil may have solidified; let re-liquefy at room temperature before proceeding.)

3 Remove steaks from marinade; allow excess marinade to drip back into baking dish. Discard excess drippings. Place steaks on gas grill directly over high heat or on charcoal grill 4 to 6 inches directly over high heat coals. Cover; grill about 7 minutes for medium-rare (preferred doneness), turning once with tongs or metal spatula. Or grill until meat thermometer inserted into thickest part of steak registers 145°F (medium-rare). Transfer steaks to plates; top each with room-temperature rosemary honey butter. Let rest 5 minutes before serving.

4 **For Butter:** In medium bowl, beat butter, rosemary, peppercorns, honey and salt with back of wooden spoon until light and fluffy. Lay 10-inch piece of plastic wrap on work surface. Mound butter mixture into center; fold plastic wrap around mixture. Roll against work surface, then between your palms into log about 3-inches long and 1 inch in diameter. (Work quickly — the butter will begin to melt.) Refrigerate wrapped log until firm, about 2 hours. Rosemary honey butter can be made in advance — store, tightly covered, in refrigerator up to 1 week.

5 Slice compound butter into 4 (1-inch) rounds; place 1 on each steak.

4 servings.

Preparation time: 12 hours, 30 minutes. Ready to serve: 12 hours, 40 minutes.

Per serving: 630 calories, 39 g total fat (16 g saturated fat), 195 mg cholesterol, 880 mg sodium, 0.5 g fiber.

BEEF TENDERLOIN

This Beef Tenderloin *recipe is so sophisticated ... and quite easy to prepare. The tenderloin is the center medallion that runs under the loin, and is perhaps the finest of beef cuts. It is costly, yes, but tender and juicy.*

½ cup (1 stick) unsalted butter, melted

5 garlic cloves, crushed

1 (3-lb.) center-cut beef tenderloin, trimmed*

2 tablespoons olive oil, plus additional for grill grate

2 tablespoons salt, preferably sea salt or kosher (coarse) salt

1 tablespoon cracked black peppercorns

1 In small bowl, mix butter and garlic. Rub tenderloin with olive oil; coat evenly with salt and peppercorns, patting gently into meat. Set aside at room temperature while preparing grill.

2 Heat grill for direct cooking.

3 Brush grill grate with oil. Place tenderloin on gas grill directly over high heat or on charcoal grill 4 to 6 inches directly over high-heat coals. Grill about 20 minutes for rare (preferred doneness), 24 for medium-rare, 29 for medium or 32 for well-done, turning occasionally and brushing frequently with prepared garlic butter. Or grill until meat thermometer inserted halfway into thickest part of tenderloin registers 140°F (rare), 145°F (medium-rare), 160°F (medium) or 170°F (well-done). Transfer tenderloin to carving board; let rest 5 minutes. Slice into rounds.

6 servings.

Preparation time: 20 minutes. Ready to serve: 40 minutes.

Per serving: 370 calories, 24 g total fat (10 g saturated fat), 115 mg cholesterol, 2410 mg sodium, 0.5 g fiber.

TIP *A center-cut beef tenderloin is the tenderloin minus the chateaubriand (large end) and the thinner "tail," as well as missing the "rope" of meat that runs just underneath the tenderloin. Although beef tenderloin has very little internal fat, all exterior fat should be trimmed before grilling. Under the fat, there's a layer of paper-thin but indigestible silver skin. To remove, slip a sharp paring knife under it and gently slice it away from the beef.

WHEN IS A STEAK DONE?

Besides using the internal temperature test, or the less-accurate "feel" test (page 18), getting a steak done to the right degree is a matter of practice and patience. There's an old Southern saying about beef: It's not done, it's not done, it's not done, it was done a minute ago, it's leather now. In other words, it's easy to undercook beef, but there's a small window when it's just right. Most professional chefs remove beef from the heat when it is five to 10 degrees cooler than the suggested temperature. The beef will continue to cook as it rests, the temperature rising accordingly.

RIB EYE STEAKS WITH A MOLE RUB

COOKING TECHNIQUE: DIRECT, HIGH HEAT

Rib eyes are made by slicing the meat off a rib roast. They come with or without bones. Rib eyes don't need to be tenderized before grilling. Instead, rub them with this Southwestern rub inspired by mole, a cocoa-spiked sauce highly prized in Tex-Mex cooking.

STEAKS

4   (10-oz.) boneless rib eye steaks, trimmed of excess fat

¼   cup olive oil, plus additional for grill grate

RUB

1   tablespoon plus 1 teaspoon chili powder

1   teaspoon packed light brown sugar

1   teaspoon each dried oregano, ground cumin, onion salt

½   teaspoon each garlic powder, unsweetened cocoa, salt, freshly ground pepper

1   **For Steaks:** Heat grill for direct cooking. Brush grill grate with oil. Rub each steak with 1 tablespoon olive oil; set aside at room temperature while preparing rub.

2   **For Rub:** In small bowl, mix chili powder, brown sugar, oregano, cumin, onion salt, garlic powder, cocoa, salt and pepper. Massage 2½ teaspoons of rub into each steak, coating bottom, top and sides.

3   Place steaks on gas grill directly over high heat or on charcoal grill 4 to 6 inches directly over high-heat coals. Cover; grill about 5 minutes for rare (preferred doneness), 6 for medium-rare, 8 for medium or 10 for well-done, turning once with tongs or metal spatula. Or grill until meat thermometer inserted into thickest part of steak registers 140°F (rare), 145°F (medium-rare), 160°F (medium) or 170°F (well-done). (For doneness, see sidebar When Is a Steak Done?, page 30.)

4 servings.

Preparation time: 20 minutes. Ready to serve: 30 minutes.

Per serving: 580 calories, 34 g total fat (9.5 g saturated fat), 160 mg cholesterol, 860 mg sodium, 1 fiber.

STEAKS, STEAKS AND MORE STEAKS

You can grill almost any steak with a simple marinade and a compound butter, as with Strip Steaks with *Rosemary Honey Butter*, page 28; or a dry rub, as here, for the rib eyes. The internal temperature guidelines remain the same. Try either method with any of these cuts: T-bone, Porterhouse, Delmonico, Sirloin or bacon-wrapped Filet Mignon.

RIB ROAST WITH GRILLED PINEAPPLE POBLANO SALSA

COOKING TECHNIQUE: DIRECT, HIGH HEAT

A standing rib roast is an easy way to make everyone happy: You slice off rib steaks for the steak lovers, carve up beef ribs for the rib crowd, and offer both to those who dither. Rib roasts, by the way, are often called "prime ribs," a bit of a misnomer because USDA-certified "prime" meat is hard for the home cook to come by.

ROAST

1 tablespoon each salt (preferably sea salt or kosher (coarse) salt), sweet paprika, freshly ground pepper

1 (3-bone, 6- to 7-lb.) rib roast, trimmed of excess fat*

SALSA

1 poblano chile (or green bell pepper, if little heat is desired in salsa)

1 medium pineapple, peeled, sliced into ½-inch-thick rings

¼ cup vegetable oil

¼ cup chopped fresh cilantro

2 tablespoons lemon juice

2 teaspoons chopped fresh mint

6 cherry tomatoes, cut into quarters

1 large shallot, minced

1 teaspoon salt

1 Heat grill for direct cooking.

2 **For Roast:** In small bowl, mix salt, paprika and pepper. Gently massage into rib roast, coating sides, top and bottom. Seal roast in aluminum foil; place bone-side down in disposable roasting pan. Set roasting pan with rib roast on gas grill directly over high heat or on charcoal grill 4 to 6 inches directly over high-heat coals. Cover; grill about 1½ hours or until meat thermometer inserted from top about halfway into roast's thickest part registers 120°F. Remove from grill. Unwrap roast — be careful of hot fat in packet. Discard pan, foil and rendered fat.

3 Place unwrapped roast bone-side down on grill grate directly over heat. If using gas grill, reduce heat to medium. If using charcoal grill, partially close lower vents and do not feed fire. Cover; grill 5 minutes. Turn onto side; grill 2 minutes. Turn onto opposite side; grill 2 additional minutes. Return roast bone-side down. Cover; grill until meat thermometer inserted halfway from top registers 140°F for rare, 145°F for medium-rare, 160°F for medium or 170°F for well-done. Finally, turn roast on top. (Be careful: The fat will ignite the flames.) Grill 1 minute or just until charred. Transfer to carving board; let rest 5 minutes.

4 To carve, slice meat off bones in one piece, leaving about ½ inch meat on bones. Carve bones apart; slice meat into ½-inch-thick rounds. Serve with salsa.

5 **For Salsa:** Heat grill for direct cooking. Place poblano chile on grill grate directly over high heat. Cook, turning often with tongs, 5 minutes or until charred. Remove from grill; seal in paper bag or place in small bowl and seal with plastic wrap. Let stand 10 minutes. Peel off blackened skin; core and seed. Chop poblano finely; place in medium bowl.

6 Brush pineapple rings with oil. Grill directly over high heat, turning once, about 6 minutes or until lightly browned. Transfer to carving board. Core slices; chop roughly. Add to bowl with poblano. Mix in cilantro, lemon juice, mint, tomatoes, shallot and salt; toss well. Serve warm or at room temperature. Salsa can be prepared ahead. Store, covered, in refrigerator up to 2 days; bring to room temperature before serving with roast.

8 servings.

Preparation time: 35 minutes. Ready to serve: 2 hours, 10 minutes.

Per serving: 485 calories, 30 g total fat (9.5 g saturated fat), 125 mg cholesterol, 1265 mg sodium, 1.5 g fiber.

TIP *Rib roasts, cut from the 6th through 12th ribs of a cow (which has 2 sets of 13 ribs), are often sold by bone count: a four-bone roast, a two-bone roast, etc. "First cut roasts" are from the ribs closer to the cow's abdomen, and are leaner and more highly prized; other cuts are fattier, closer to the chuck. Although large strips of fat should be trimmed, rib roasts should nonetheless retain a layer of top fat for protection. If desired, the bones can also be "frenched" — that is, the meat can be trimmed, exposing about half of each rib. It's a tricky technique, designed for a fancy presentation — ask your butcher to do it for you.

TEXAS BRISKET WITH A CLASSIC TEXAS BARBECUE SAUCE

All around Austin, Texas, brisket fosters turf wars. Sweet sauces, vinegar sauces, slow-roasted, spit-roasted: These are terms of the battle. But no matter how you slice it, barbecued brisket is, as they say in the Lone Star State, "one fine meal." This spicy, beer-drenched, big-flavored sauce would also work well with pork loin or any game meat.

BRISKET

- 1 (5- to 6-lb.) beef brisket*
- 2 tablespoons chili powder
- 1 tablespoon each sweet paprika, packed light brown sugar, salt, preferably sea salt or kosher (coarse) salt
- 2 teaspoons freshly ground pepper
- 4 cups wood chips, soaked at least 3 hours or preferably overnight, then drained
- 1 (12-oz.) bottle beer, preferably wheat beer or summer ale, at room temperature

BARBECUE SAUCE

- 1 (15-oz.) can tomato sauce
- ¼ cup each ketchup, chili sauce, cider vinegar, bread-and-butter pickle juice
- 2 tablespoons packed dark brown sugar
- 1 teaspoon onion salt
- ½ teaspoon crushed red pepper
- ¼ teaspoon garlic powder
- 1 dried ancho chile, cored and seeded, ground in spice grinder or coffee grinder; or 1½ tablespoons dried ancho chile powder

1 **For Brisket:** Cover work surface with large sheet of plastic wrap. Rinse brisket; pat dry with paper towels. Place on plastic wrap. In small bowl, combine chili powder, paprika, brown sugar, salt and pepper; massage into all sides of brisket. Cover in plastic wrap; refrigerate at least 8 hours but no more than 24 hours. Bring to room temperature before barbecuing.

2 Arrange grill for indirect cooking with drip pan under unheated portion of grill grate. Heat grill. If using gas grill, place wood chips in smoker box. Or place chips in small heavy-duty disposable aluminum pan or metal loaf pan, placing pan directly on lava rocks. If using charcoal grill, scatter chips on coals or place in disposable pan set directly on coals. Allow chips to begin to smoke, about 10 minutes.

3 Place brisket on gas grill over drip pan, indirectly over medium heat; or on charcoal grill over drip pan, but to the side of medium-hot coals. Cover; barbecue, mopping with beer every 30 minutes, 5 to 6 hours or until tender when pierced with dinner fork.

4 **Meanwhile, for Sauce:** In medium saucepan, bring tomato sauce, ketchup, chili sauce, vinegar and pickle juice to a simmer over medium-high heat. Stir in brown sugar, onion salt, crushed red pepper, garlic powder and ancho chile. Reduce heat to medium-low; simmer 20 minutes or until thickened, stirring occasionally. If desired, sauce can be made on grill in heavy-duty saucepan directly over medium heat. If so, make sauce before brisket begins to cook so grill's lid is not lifted too often.

5 When brisket is done, transfer to carving board, using 2 large spatulas or grilling gloves. Let rest 20 minutes.** Carve into ½-inch-thick strips. Serve with sauce.

10 servings.

Preparation time: 8 hours, 40 minutes. Ready to serve: 14 hours.

Per serving: 330 calories, 13 g total fat (5 g saturated fat), 100 mg cholesterol, 1400 sodium, 2 g fiber.

TIP *Because the brisket roasts for so long, don't trim the top layer of fat. This will protect the meat, melting as it cooks. Texas brisket, of course, is actually done in a smoker — but this method is as close as you can get in a conventional grill to the smokehouse taste.

TIP **If you like less crunch in your brisket, wrap it loosely in aluminum foil when it comes off the grill. Set aside 30 minutes before carving.

TEXAS SIDES

In Texas, brisket is traditionally served on parchment paper or waxed paper sheets spread out at each diner's place. Plates are considered too fussy for barbecue in the Lone Star State. The brisket is accompanied by minced onions, pickled jalapeños, dill pickle spears and thick slices of plain white bread. Fancier meals would include *Baked Beans* (page 144).

CHILI ON THE GRILL

There's no need to heat up the kitchen — make Chili on the Grill! *The vegetables are fire-roasted, then stirred into the stew, which is cooked in a pot placed directly on the grill grate. Use a heavy pot, preferably cast iron.*

1	medium eggplant
2	teaspoons salt
1	large onion, sliced into ½-inch-thick rings
1	green bell pepper, quartered
¼	cup plus 2 tablespoons olive oil, plus additional for grill grate
1	lb. lean ground beef
2	garlic cloves, minced
¼	cup chili powder
½	teaspoon ground cinnamon
½	teaspoon ground cumin
1	(28-oz.) can diced tomatoes or whole tomatoes, diced, undrained
1	(12-oz.) bottle beer, preferably summer wheat or pale ale

1 Slice eggplant into 1-inch-thick rings; sprinkle ½ teaspoon of the salt over all slices. Place in colander in sink; drain 30 minutes. Meanwhile, heat grill for direct cooking.

2 Blot eggplant slices dry with paper towels. In large bowl, toss eggplant, onion and bell pepper with ¼ cup of the olive oil.

3 Brush grill grate with oil. Place vegetables on gas grill directly over medium heat or on charcoal grill 4 to 6 inches directly over medium-heat coals. Grill, turning once with metal spatula, about 7 minutes or until softened and brown. Remove from grill; roughly chop.

4 In large pot, preferably cast iron, heat remaining 2 tablespoons olive oil on grill grate directly over medium heat. Add ground beef and garlic; stir. Cover grill; cook 5 minutes or until meat is sizzling and no longer pink. Stir in chili powder, cinnamon and cumin; cook 20 seconds or until fragrant, stirring constantly. Stir in tomatoes (with their juice), beer and chopped grilled vegetables. Cover grill (not pot); cook, stirring frequently, 45 minutes or until slightly thickened. Season with remaining 1½ teaspoons salt.

6 servings.

Preparation time: 50 minutes. Ready to serve: 1 hour, 50 minutes.

Per serving: 375 calories, 25 g total fat (6.5 g saturated fat), 45 mg cholesterol, 935 mg sodium, 6.5 g fiber.

BEEF RIBS WITH A PLUM BARBECUE SAUCE

Beef ribs are meatier than pork ribs, so they benefit from indirect, long cooking, during which the meat becomes extraordinarily tender and pulls away from the bones. The Plum Barbecue Sauce that matches these ribs is sweet and aromatic.

PLUM BARBECUE SAUCE

1   medium onion, finely chopped

2   tablespoons minced peeled fresh ginger

1   (15-oz.) can tomato sauce

½   cup plum preserves or jam

½   cup reduced-sodium beef broth or water

¼   cup dark rum

2   tablespoons Dijon mustard

2   tablespoons sherry vinegar or red wine vinegar

2   tablespoons Worcestershire sauce

⅛   teaspoon ground cloves

RIBS

3   cups wood chips or chunks, soaked in water 3 hours or overnight, then drained

2   (3-lb.) racks beef ribs

1 **For Sauce:** In medium saucepan, bring onion, ginger, tomato sauce, preserves, broth, rum, Dijon, vinegar, Worcestershire and cloves to a simmer over medium-high heat. Reduce heat to low; simmer uncovered 20 minutes or until slightly thickened, stirring occasionally. If desired, sauce can be made directly on grill in heavy-duty saucepan set directly over medium heat.

2 **For Ribs:** Arrange grill for indirect cooking with drip pan under unheated portion of grill grate. Heat grill. If using gas grill, place wood chips in smoker box; or place chips in small heavy-duty disposable aluminum pan or metal loaf pan, placing pan directly on lava rocks. If using charcoal grill, scatter chips on coals or place in disposable pan set directly on coals. Allow chips to begin to smoke, about 10 minutes.

3 Place ribs meat-side down on gas grill over drip pan, indirectly over high heat or on charcoal grill over drip pan, but to the side of high-heat coals. Cover; barbecue, mopping frequently with barbecue sauce and turning occasionally, 1½ to 2 hours or until ribs are mahogany and meat pulls back from bones. Transfer to carving board; let stand 5 minutes. Carve between ribs to serve.

4 servings.

Preparation time: 40 minutes. Ready to serve: 2 hours, 45 minutes.

Per serving: 940 calories, 47 g total fat (17.5 g saturated fat), 245 mg cholesterol, 1045 mg sodium, 3 g fiber.

MIDWESTERN HAMBURGERS

These are the classic burgers, the ones your family will come back for again and again. They were inspired by the "Butter Burgers" that Culver's Frozen Custard restaurants have made famous across the upper Midwest — admittedly, about the best burgers we can imagine. Freeze the butter overnight so it's firm enough to dice and cut into the meat.

1½ lb. lean ground beef

2 teaspoons salt

1 teaspoon freshly ground pepper

¼ cup (½ stick) unsalted butter, diced, frozen 2 hours

Vegetable oil for grill grate, plus additional for buns

4 hamburger buns, halved

8 green onions

4 hamburger buns, halved

1 Heat grill for direct cooking.

2 Place beef, salt and pepper in large bowl. Quickly cut butter into meat and seasonings with 2 forks or pastry cutter just until well distributed, not until melted. Form mixture into 4 (5-inch) patties.

3 Brush grill grate with oil. Place burgers on gas grill directly over high heat or on charcoal grill 4 to 6 inches directly over high-heat coals. Cover; grill, turning once, 9 to 11 minutes or until cooked through.* Transfer to carving board; let rest while grilling green onions and buns.

4 Place green onions on grill grate directly over high heat. Cook, turning once, 4 minutes or until wilted and charred. Transfer to carving board; slice into 4-inch segments.

5 Brush cut side of buns with oil; place on grill grate cut-side down directly over high heat. Toast about 1 minute. Serve burgers on buns with green onions and condiments of your choice.

4 servings.

Preparation time: 15 minutes. Ready to serve: 30 minutes.

Per serving: 465 calories, 35 g total fat (16 g saturated fat), 125 mg cholesterol, 1245 mg sodium, 1 g fiber.

TIP *Don't press the patties with a spatula as they cook. If you do, you'll press out the butter, defeating the purpose of these ultimate burgers. According to USDA guidelines, ground beef should be cooked until well-done or until meat thermometer inserted into burger registers 170°F. If you're concerned about having a juicy burger, remember the butter.

FAJITAS IN A SANGRIA MARINADE

These build-your-own wraps are perfect for picnics or backyard get-togethers.

SANGRIA MARINADE

1   cup red wine
2/3 cup carbonated lemon-lime soda
3   tablespoons orange juice
1½ tablespoons brandy
1   tablespoon lime juice
1   (4-inch) cinnamon stick
6   allspice berries
2   lb. or 2 (1-lb.) skirt steak(s)

FAJITAS

2   large onions, sliced into ½-inch-thick rings
2   large green bell peppers, cut into ½-inch-long strips
5   tablespoons olive oil, plus additional for grill grate
1   tablespoon salt
1½ teaspoons freshly ground pepper
16 flour tortillas
1   (8-oz.) container sour cream
1   medium jar hot salsa

GUACAMOLE

3   large, ripe avocados, peeled, pitted
1   large tomato, coarsely chopped
1   small red onion, minced
1   pickled jalapeño chile, stemmed, seeded and minced
3   tablespoons lime juice
½   teaspoon each garlic powder, salt, freshly ground pepper
4   drops hot pepper sauce or to taste

1 For Marinade: In medium bowl, mix together all ingredients except steak. Place steak(s) in large baking dish. Pour marinade over meat; turn to coat. Cover; refrigerate at least 4 hours but no more than 10 hours, turning occasionally.

2 For Fajitas: Heat grill for direct cooking. In medium bowl, toss onions and bell peppers with 2 tablespoons of the olive oil, 1 teaspoon of the salt and ½ teaspoon of the ground pepper. Remove meat from marinade; discard marinade. Sprinkle steak(s) with remaining 2 teaspoons salt and 1 teaspoon ground pepper. Let rest at room temperature as grill heats.

3 Brush grill grate with oil. Place steak(s) on gas grill directly over high heat or on charcoal grill 4 to 6 inches directly over high-heat coals. Cover; grill 7 minutes, turning once. Transfer to carving board; let rest 5 minutes. Place vegetables on grill directly over high heat. Cover; grill about 4 minutes, turning once. Transfer to serving platter. Place tortillas on grill directly over high heat. Grill, turning once, 30 seconds or until warm and softened. Remove to serving platter. Cut steak into ¼-inch slices against the grain. Serve by rolling steak slices into tortillas with grilled vegetables, sour cream, salsa and guacamole.

4 For Guacamole: In large bowl, mash avocados with fork. Mix in tomato and remaining ingredients; stir until well blended. Cover; refrigerate until ready to serve.

8 servings.

Preparation time: 4 hours, 45 minutes. Ready to serve: 5 hours.

Per serving: 615 calories, 30 g total fat (5.5 g saturated fat), 45 mg cholesterol, 1655 mg sodium, 8.5 g fiber.

LONDON BROIL

Surprisingly, there's no such thing as a London Broil. *At least, there's no cut of meat named "London Broil." Rather, it's a way to cook and (most importantly) slice top or bottom round, which is a chewy but tasty cut. To tenderize the beef, marinate it in a lemony vinaigrette before giving it a lemon-pepper crust.*

MARINADE
½ cup olive oil
¼ cup lemon juice
1 tablespoon minced peeled fresh ginger
2 teaspoons soy sauce
1 teaspoon sugar

BEEF
2 lb. top (preferably) or bottom round, trimmed of excess fat
1 tablespoon lemon pepper seasoning
Vegetable oil for grill grate

1 **For Marinade:** In small bowl, whisk olive oil, lemon juice, ginger, soy sauce and sugar until blended. Place beef in medium baking dish. Pour marinade over beef; turn to coat. Cover; refrigerate at least 2 hours but no more than 6 hours, turning occasionally.

2 Heat grill for direct cooking. Let beef and marinade come to room temperature while grill heats.

3 **For Beef:** Remove beef from marinade; discard marinade. Gently blot beef dry with paper towels. Sprinkle lemon pepper over top, bottom and sides; pat to create coating.

4 Brush grill grate with oil. Place beef on gas grill directly over high heat or on charcoal grill 4 to 6 inches directly over high-heat coals. Cover; grill 5 minutes for rare, 6 for medium-rare, 8 for medium or 10 for well-done, turning once. Or grill until meat thermometer inserted halfway into thickest part of steak registers 140°F (rare), 145°F (medium-rare), 160°F (medium) or 170°F (well-done).

5 Transfer London Broil to carving board; let stand 5 minutes. Slice into ⅛-inch-thick slices against the grain and on the bias by cutting with sharp carving knife positioned at a 45-degree angle to the carving board. Do not saw. Rather, draw knife firmly but evenly across steak to slice.

4 servings.

Preparation time: 4 hours, 15 minutes. Ready to serve: 4 hours, 25 minutes.

Per serving: 300 calories, 13 g total fat (3 g saturated fat), 110 mg cholesterol, 385 mg sodium, 0 g fiber.

INSIDE-OUT CHEESEBURGERS

Everyone likes cheeseburgers! But they're a mess on the grill. So put the cheese inside the patties! Let these burgers rest a few minutes before serving, because the cheese superheats, the way it does on a pizza.

¼ cup (1 oz.) shredded cheddar cheese, at room temperature

¼ cup (1 oz.) crumbled blue cheese, preferably Gorgonzola, at room temperature

1½ lb. lean ground beef

1 tablespoon plus 1 teaspoon Worcestershire sauce

1 teaspoon sweet paprika

Vegetable oil for grill grate, plus additional for buns

4 hamburger buns, halved

1 Heat grill for direct cooking. In small bowl, mix cheddar cheese and blue cheese. In large bowl, mix ground beef, Worcestershire and paprika with wooden spoon until uniform. Divide into 8 equal portions. Place on parchment paper; flatten each into 4-inch-long round, ¼ inch thick. Spread one-fourth of cheese mixture (about 2 tablespoons) onto each of 4 patties, leaving ½-inch border around edges. Cover each with remaining patty, crimping edges so cheese won't leak when grilled. Pat to seal.

2 Brush grill grate with oil. Place patties on gas grill directly over high heat or on charcoal grill 4 to 6 inches directly over high-heat coals. Grill, turning once with metal spatula, 8 to 10 minutes or until cooked through. Transfer to carving board; let rest 5 minutes. Brush cut side of buns with oil; place on grill grate, cut-side down, over high heat. Toast about 1 minute or until browned. Serve burgers on buns with condiments of your choice.

4 servings.

Preparation time: 20 minutes. Ready to serve: 30 minutes.

Per serving: 415 calories, 30 g total fat (12.5 g saturated fat), 110 mg cholesterol, 285 mg sodium, 0 g fiber.

CHEESEBURGER VARIATIONS

Mix one of the following into the cheese mixture before it's placed on the patties:

2 tablespoons crumbled cooked bacon or bacon-flavored bits

1 tablespoon dehydrated minced onion

1 tablespoon fresh thyme

2 teaspoons finely chopped roasted peanuts

2 teaspoons finely chopped toasted hazelnuts or walnuts

½ teaspoon garlic powder

4 drops hot pepper sauce

1 green onion, finely minced

Or finely shred or crumble any one of the following cheeses and substitute it for Gorgonzola: Asiago, Boursin, Brie, Buffalo mozzarella, Monterey Jack, Parmesan, Provolone, Roblechon, soft goat cheese or Swiss.

VIETNAMESE GRILLED BEEF SALAD

This traditional Vietnamese dish is served in lettuce cups with roasted peanuts and aromatic herbs. For an even more authentic presentation, roll the filling inside the lettuce leaves before you eat it, like an egg roll.

MARINADE

1 (12-oz.) can ginger ale
¼ cup fish sauce
¼ cup lime juice
1½ teaspoons freshly ground pepper
3 green onions, minced
2 garlic cloves, crushed
1 (1½-lb.) boneless sirloin steak, pricked all over with fork

SALAD

¼ cup chopped roasted peanuts
¼ cup chopped fresh cilantro
¼ cup thinly sliced radishes
2 tablespoons chopped fresh mint
2 tablespoons rice vinegar
2 teaspoons sesame oil
2 teaspoons soy sauce
1 head Bibb lettuce, leaves torn off to make cups

1 **For Marinade:** In medium bowl, mix ginger ale, fish sauce, lime juice, pepper, green onions and garlic. Place steak in large baking dish. Pour marinade over steak; turn to coat. Cover; refrigerate at least 2 hours but no more than 5 hours, turning occasionally.

2 Heat grill for direct cooking. Drain marinade from steak; discard marinade. Let meat sit at room temperature while grill heats.

3 Place steak on gas grill directly over high heat or on charcoal grill 4 to 6 inches directly over high-heat coals. Cover; grill about 7 minutes for rare, 8 for medium-rare (preferred doneness) or 10 minutes for medium, turning once. Or grill until meat thermometer inserted into thickest part of steak registers 140°F (rare), 145°F (medium-rare) or 160°F (medium). (Well-done is not recommended.) Transfer to carving board; let rest 5 minutes. Slice into ⅛-inch strips against the grain.

4 **For Salad:** Place steak strips in large bowl. Toss with peanuts, cilantro, radishes, mint, vinegar, sesame oil and soy sauce. Serve in lettuce cups.

6 servings.

Preparation time: 2 hours, 30 minutes. Ready to serve: 2 hours, 40 minutes.

Per serving: 190 calories, 7.5 g total fat (2 g saturated fat), 60 mg cholesterol, 205 mg sodium, 1 g fiber.

STUFFED FLANK STEAK WITH A HOISIN MARINADE

COOKING TECHNIQUE: DIRECT, MEDIUM HEAT

*Here's a truly international dish — an American barbecue take on Japanese green onion-stuffed steak rolls (*negimaki*) — flavored here with an aromatic Chinese-inspired marinade. If you don't want to go to the trouble of making a pocket in the steak, ask your butcher to do it for you.*

STEAKS

1   (1¾-lb.) flank steak
8   thin asparagus spears*
8   green onions

MARINADE

¼   cup dry vermouth or white wine
¼   cup soy sauce
3   tablespoons hoisin sauce**
2   tablespoons orange juice
2   tablespoons minced peeled fresh ginger
1   tablespoon rice vinegar
½   teaspoon chili oil or hot pepper sauce
1   garlic clove, crushed
     Vegetable oil for grill grate

1   To cut pocket in flank steak, make long narrow incision in thicker, longer side of steak using sharp chef's knife. Flip steak over and deepen incision by slicing farther into meat. Keep flipping and slicing until pocket is formed — do not cut through to opposite side but leave ½ inch of meat on the three remaining sides to hold pocket together. Slice gently to minimize tearing.

2   Trim asparagus and green onions to fit pocket. Place in pocket lengthwise (parallel to incision), alternating directions. Tie steak with butcher twine at 3-inch increments, perpendicular to asparagus spears and green onions. Place in large loaf pan or in medium baking dish.

3   **For Marinade:** In small bowl, whisk vermouth, soy sauce, hoisin, orange juice, ginger, rice vinegar, chili oil and garlic until blended. Reserve one-fourth of the marinade. Pour remaining marinade over stuffed steak; turn to coat. Cover; refrigerate at least 2 hours but no more than 6 hours, turning occasionally.

4   Heat grill for direct cooking. Remove meat from marinade; discard marinade. Bring meat to room temperature as grill heats. Brush grill grate with oil. Place stuffed steak on gas grill directly over medium heat or on charcoal grill 4 to 6 inches directly over medium-hot coals. Cover; grill about 20 minutes for medium-rare or 26 minutes for medium, turning and basting frequently with reserved marinade until browned all over. Transfer to carving board; let stand 5 minutes.

5   Slice off 1 piece of butcher twine. Then carve on the bias by placing knife at a 45-degree angle to cutting surface, drawing it evenly and slowly across steak and vegetables. Cut off remaining pieces of twine only as you reach them while slicing.

4 servings.

Preparation time: 2 hours, 20 minutes. Ready to serve: 2 hours, 35 minutes.

Per serving: 320 calories, 13.5 g total fat (5 g saturated fat), 105 mg cholesterol, 355 mg sodium, 1.5 g fiber.

TIP *Buy asparagus spears only ¼ inch in diameter. If you can't find them this thin, either peel them down to this diameter using vegetable peeler, or blanch them in skillet of boiling water 1 minute before stuffing them in the flank steak.

TIP **Hoisin sauce is a Chinese condiment made from soybeans, sugar, vinegar and spices. Typically, it's written as one word in the West ("hoisin"), although it is indeed two words in Chinese. Chee hou sauce is a stronger version of hoisin. Substitute it in any recipe for a more pungent taste.

Bourbon Baby Back Ribs with a Maple Barbecue Sauce, page 59

PORK

Few meats lend themselves to the grill better than pork. From ribs to sausages, loins to chops, pork makes backyard cooking a success. What's more, today's pork is less fatty than ever — and more flavorful. Some chops are even leaner than chicken breasts. It's hard to ruin pork — unless you overcook it, always a danger with leaner cuts. True, you don't want to eat pink pork, but there's a fine line between done and overdone. Watch the temperatures and times carefully as you prepare these meals.

PORK CHOPS STUFFED WITH GRILLED APPLE CHUTNEY

Since there's no better combination than apples and pork, these chops are stuffed with a Grilled Apple Chutney. You can also make this apple chutney on its own, a great accompaniment for grilled chicken, turkey or game fowls.

CHOPS

4 (10- to 12-oz.) 1-inch-thick rib pork chops

3 tablespoons plus 1 teaspoon vegetable oil, plus additional for grill grate

2 teaspoons garam masala*

CHUTNEY

2 tart firm baking apples, peeled, cored and sliced ½ inch thick

1 small onion, minced

1 garlic clove, minced

1 tablespoon minced peeled fresh ginger

1 tablespoon packed light brown sugar

1½ teaspoons cider vinegar

2 tablespoons A-1 steak sauce

½ teaspoon each salt, freshly ground pepper

1 Heat grill for direct cooking.

2 **For Chops:** Cut pockets in chops by inserting paring knife in side of chops opposite bones. Slice evenly and gently, all the way to the bone, taking care not to cut through ends of chops. Rub each chop with 1 teaspoon of the oil and ½ teaspoon garam masala. Cover; refrigerate while preparing chutney.

3 **For Chutney:** In medium bowl, toss apples with 1 tablespoon of the oil. Place slices on gas grill directly over high heat or on charcoal grill 4 to 6 inches directly over high-heat coals. Cover; grill, turning once, about 4 minutes or until lightly browned. Transfer to carving board; roughly chop.

4 Heat remaining 1 tablespoon oil in heavy medium saucepan or in pan placed on grill grate directly over high heat. Add onion, garlic and ginger; sauté 5 minutes or until onion softens, stirring occasionally. Add brown sugar and vinegar; simmer 1 minute, stirring constantly. Stir in chopped apples, steak sauce, salt and pepper; simmer 2 minutes. Remove from heat to cool completely.

5 Stuff ⅓ cup chutney into pocket of each chop. Place chops on gas grill directly over high heat or on charcoal grill 4 to 6 inches directly over high-heat coals. Cover; grill 10 minutes or until meat is no longer pink, turning once using 2 spatulas if necessary. Do not press down on chops while grilling. Transfer to carving board; let stand 5 minutes before serving.

4 servings.

Preparation time: 1 hour. Ready to serve: 1 hour, 45 minutes.

Per serving: 450 calories, 25 g total fat (6.5 g saturated fat), 110 mg cholesterol, 475 mg sodium, 2 g fiber.

TIP *Garam masala is a blend of as many as 12 spices, including ground cinnamon, cloves and cumin. It's available in the spice rack of most supermarkets.

STUFFED PORK LOIN

This Stuffed Pork Loin *taps the tastes of Germany. The only change: Gin replaces the juniper berries, which traditionally spice the sauerkraut. If you want, have your butcher butterfly the pork loin for you. Another option: Mop the loin with room-temperature dark beer during its last 30 minutes on the grill.*

1	(1-lb.) pkg. fresh sauerkraut, drained, squeezed of excess moisture
2	tablespoons Dijon mustard
1	tablespoon caraway seeds
1	tablespoon gin
1	(4- to 4½-lb.) boneless pork loin, butterflied
1	lb. thick-sliced bacon

1 In medium bowl, mix sauerkraut, Dijon, caraway seeds and gin. Lay pork loin cut-side up on work surface. Spread sauerkraut mixture down center of loin; fold to close. Place stuffed loin fat-side down on work surface. Lay bacon over meat, overlapping strips by half. Tie with butcher twine to secure bacon and seal stuffing. Set aside at room temperature while grill heats.

2 Arrange grill for indirect cooking with drip pan under unheated portion of grill grate. Heat grill.

3 Place stuffed loin bacon-side up on gas grill over drip pan, indirectly over medium heat; or on charcoal grill over drip pan, but to the side of medium-hot coals. Cover; barbecue 3 hours or until meat thermometer inserted into meat (but not touching stuffing) registers 160°F for medium (the preferred doneness) or 170°F for well-done.

4 Move loin over direct medium heat; grill, turning once, 3 minutes or until brown.

5 Transfer to carving board; let rest 5 minutes. Slice off butcher twine. Carve into ¾-inch slices.

10 servings.

Preparation time: 30 minutes. Ready to serve: 3 hours, 30 minutes.

Per serving: 390 calories, 20.5 g total fat (7 g saturated fat), 125 mg cholesterol, 780 mg sodium, 2 g fiber.

TUSCAN GRILLED PORK LOIN

Legend has it that the aromatic Tuscan countryside drove people to cook over open fires. Nothing represents the ideal of Tuscan cooking (and the essence of easy grilling) better than this simple, flavorful Tuscan Grilled Pork Loin.

1   (2½- to 3-lb.) boneless pork loin roast

6   garlic cloves, sliced into quarters

2   tablespoons olive oil, plus additional for grill grate

5   tablespoons chopped fresh rosemary

1   tablespoon grated lemon peel, minced

2   teaspoons salt, preferably sea salt or kosher (coarse) salt

2   teaspoons freshly ground pepper

1 Make 24 (½-inch deep) slits all over pork loin roast. Slip 1 garlic quarter in each slit. Rub olive oil over roast.

2 In small bowl, combine rosemary, lemon peel, salt and pepper. Place large sheet of parchment paper on work surface; pour herb mixture onto sheet. Roll roast in herbs, coating all sides and gently pressing mixture onto surface. Wrap in second, clean sheet of parchment paper. If desired, also seal in plastic wrap or large resealable plastic bag. Refrigerate at least 4 hours but no more than 24 hours.

3 Arrange grill for indirect cooking with drip pan under unheated portion of grill grate. Heat grill. Unwrap pork loin; press herbs that fall off back onto meat. Let stand at room temperature while grill heats.

4 Brush grill grate with oil. Place pork loin on gas grill over drip pan, indirectly over medium heat; or on charcoal grill over drip pan, to the side of medium-hot coals. Cover; barbecue, turning occasionally, 1 to 1½ hours or until well browned and meat thermometer inserted halfway into thickest part of loin registers 160°F for medium (preferred doneness) or 170°F for well done. Transfer to carving board; let stand 5 minutes. Carve into thin rounds.

4 servings.

Preparation time: 45 minutes. Ready to serve: 2 hours.

Per serving: 540 calories, 30 g total fat (8.5 g saturated fat), 180 mg cholesterol, 1275 mg sodium, 1 g fiber.

JERK LOIN

Jamaican jerk barbecue is traditionally fiery, eye-watering and cooked in a steel drum. This moderated version has been adapted for your backyard cookout.

JERK RUB

1   small onion, minced

6   green onions, minced

2   garlic cloves, minced

6   tablespoons canola or vegetable oil, plus additional for grill grate

2   tablespoons cider vinegar

2   tablespoons dark rum

2   teaspoons packed dark brown sugar

1   habanero or fresh jalapeño chile, stemmed, seeded and finely chopped

1   tablespoon minced peeled fresh ginger

1   tablespoon plus 1 teaspoon salt

2   teaspoons ground allspice

2   teaspoons fresh thyme

½   teaspoon ground cinnamon

½   teaspoon grated nutmeg

ROAST

1   (2½- to 3-lb.) boneless pork loin roast

3   ripe plantains, peeled

1   **For Rub:** In medium bowl, mix onion, green onions and garlic. Stir in 3 tablespoons of the oil, vinegar, rum and brown sugar until uniform. Stir in chile, ginger, 1 tablespoon of the salt, allspice, thyme, cinnamon and nutmeg until paste-like. Place loin in large resealable plastic bag. Pour in rub. Seal bag; massage rub into pork. Refrigerate at least 4 hours but no more than 10 hours.

2   Arrange grill for indirect cooking with drip pan under unheated portion of grill grate. Heat grill. Remove loin from marinade; discard marinade. Pat any spices that have fallen off back onto meat. Let stand at room temperature while grill heats.

3   **For Roast:** Brush grill grate with oil. Place pork loin on gas grill over drip pan, indirectly over medium heat; or on charcoal grill over drip pan, but to the side of medium-hot coals. Cover; barbecue 1 hour.

4   Meanwhile, slice plantains, first lengthwise, then into halves. Place in medium bowl; toss with 3 tablespoons oil and remaining 1 teaspoon salt.

5   Move loin directly over medium heat; grill, turning on all 4 sides, about 20 minutes or until coating is crunchy and meat thermometer inserted halfway into thickest part of loin registers 160°F for medium (preferred doneness) or 170°F for well-done. Transfer to carving board; let stand 10 minutes.

6   Meanwhile, place plantains directly over medium heat; grill, turning once, 6 minutes or until browned. Carve loin into thin rounds; serve with plantains.

6 servings.

Preparation time: 1 hour. Ready to serve: 5 hours, 40 minutes.

Per serving: 605 calories, 30 g total fat (6 g saturated fat), 120 mg cholesterol, 1635 mg sodium, 4 g fiber.

TEQUILA-BRINED PORK CHOPS

You wouldn't normally brine pork chops (soak them in a salt solution to seal in the juices) because they're a relatively fatty cut of meat. But doing so lets them sit on the grill longer, absorbing more smoky flavors.

4 (10-oz.) boneless center-cut loin pork chops
1½ cups tequila
1 cup water
¼ cup salt
1 tablespoon sugar
4 garlic cloves, thinly sliced
2 tablespoons cumin seeds, crushed*
1 tablespoon mustard seeds, crushed*
3 bay leaves
½ teaspoon crushed red pepper (optional)

1 Place pork chops in large resealable plastic bag. In medium bowl, whisk tequila, water, salt and sugar until salt dissolves; pour into bag with chops. Add garlic, cumin seed, mustard seeds, bay leaves and crushed red pepper, if using. Seal bag; shake to coat chops. Refrigerate at least 6 hours but no more than 24 hours. Shake bag occasionally to redistribute marinade.

2 Arrange grill for indirect cooking with drip pan under unheated portion of grill grate. Heat grill. Let chops and marinade stand at room temperature while grill heats.

3 Remove chops from marinade; discard marinade. Do not blot chops dry. Place on gas grill over drip pan, indirectly over medium heat; or on charcoal grill over drip pan, but to the side of medium-hot coals. Cover; cook 15 minutes.

4 Move chops directly over medium heat. Cook, turning once, about 6 minutes or until browned and meat thermometer inserted into thickest part of chop registers 160°F for medium or 170°F for well-done. Let stand 5 minutes before serving.

4 servings.

Preparation time: 20 minutes. Ready to serve: 6 hours, 45 minutes.

Per serving: 480 calories, 22 g total fat (7.5 g saturated fat), 175 mg cholesterol, 1855 mg sodium, 0.5 g fiber.

TIP *To crush cumin and mustard seeds, place them between 2 sheets of parchment paper. Crimp edges so seeds don't roll out, and gently press down with large, heavy saucepan.

CHINESE SPARE RIBS

COOKING TECHNIQUE: DIRECT, HIGH HEAT

Chinese Spare Ribs *are certainly a take-out favorite, but here's an easy 3-step technique for making them at home: Boil them to get rid of excess fat, steam them in a foil packet on the grill, then char them over high heat.*

CHINESE BARBECUE SAUCE

½ cup hoisin sauce (see TIP, page 47)

½ cup soy sauce

½ cup dry sherry

2 tablespoons ketchup

2 tablespoons chili sauce

2 tablespoons rice vinegar

2 tablespoons minced peeled fresh ginger

½ teaspoon five-spice powder

1 green onion, finely minced

1 garlic clove, crushed

RIBS

2 (3-lb.) pork spare rib racks*

1 For Sauce: In medium bowl, whisk hoisin, soy sauce, sherry, ketchup, chili sauce, rice vinegar, ginger, five-spice powder, green onion and garlic until blended. Sauce can be prepared ahead. Store, covered, in refrigerator up to 5 days; bring to room temperature before using.

2 For Ribs: Fill large pot or Dutch oven halfway with water; bring to a boil over high heat. Add rib racks; cook 5 minutes. Drain; cool slightly. Meanwhile, heat grill for direct cooking. Wrap ribs in aluminum foil; seal tightly. Place on gas grill directly over high heat or on charcoal grill 4 to 6 inches directly over high-heat coals. Cover; cook 30 minutes. Unwrap packet, remove rib racks and discard fat and foil. (Be careful — rendered fat is very hot.) Return racks

meat-side down to grill directly over high heat. Mop with Chinese Barbecue Sauce; grill, turning once and mopping frequently with sauce, 10 minutes or until sizzling and browned. Transfer to carving board; let stand 5 minutes. Carve between ribs to serve. Serve with extra sauce.

4 servings.

Preparation time: 30 minutes. Ready to serve: 1 hour.

Per serving: 590 calories, 41 g total fat (15 g saturated fat), 160 mg cholesterol, 1245 mg sodium, 1 g fiber.

TIP *Like baby backs, pork spare ribs sometimes have a membrane running down the back of the ribs. Peel this paper-thin strip off by hand, starting at the smallest bone and pulling to the largest with a gentle, firm pressure. Or have your butcher do it for you.

BOURBON BABY BACK RIBS WITH A MAPLE BARBECUE SAUCE

Right off, it must be said that baby back ribs are not from a baby pig. They're the small loin ribs, those from the upper end of the rib cage. Baby backs are best with a simple, smoky marinade — here, just good Kentucky bourbon.

RIBS

- 1 (750-ml) bottle bourbon
- ½ teaspoon liquid smoke seasoning (optional)
- 2 (1-lb.) racks baby back ribs, trimmed

MAPLE BARBECUE SAUCE

- 2 tablespoons olive oil, plus additional for grill grate
- 1 large onion, chopped
- ½ cup ketchup
- ½ cup plus 1 tablespoon cider vinegar
- ¼ cup chili sauce
- ¼ cup lime juice
- ¼ cup maple syrup
- 1 tablespoon Worcestershire sauce
- 1 tablespoon dry mustard
- ⅛ teaspoon ground cloves
- 6 drops hot pepper sauce (optional)

1 **For Ribs:** Reserve ¼ cup bourbon. Pour remainder into large baking dish; mix in liquid smoke, if using. Lay ribs meat-side down in marinade. Cover; refrigerate at least 4 hours or up to 24 hours, turning occasionally.

2 **For Sauce:** In medium saucepan, heat olive oil over medium heat until hot. Add onion; cook 3 minutes or until tender, stirring frequently. Stir in ketchup, vinegar, chili sauce, lime juice, maple syrup, Worcestershire, mustard, cloves, reserved ¼ cup bourbon and hot pepper sauce, if using. Simmer uncovered 25 minutes or until slightly thickened, stirring occasionally. Sauce can also be made on grill: Place heavy-duty medium saucepan on grill grate directly over medium heat. Sauce can be prepared ahead. Refrigerate, covered, up to 4 days; bring to room temperature before using.

3 Bring ribs and marinade to room temperature while grill heats. Arrange grill for indirect cooking with drip pan under unheated portion of grill grate. Heat grill.

4 Remove ribs from marinade; discard marinade. Place meat-side down on gas grill over drip pan, but indirectly over medium heat; or on charcoal grill over drip pan, but to the side of medium-hot coals. Brush with sauce. Cover; barbecue 40 minutes, basting every 10 minutes with sauce. Turn; barbecue, basting every 10 minutes with sauce, 1 hour or until meat pulls back from bones. If you want crispier ribs, transfer directly over heat or coals for last 5 minutes of cooking. Turn ribs once to let marinade crisp over heat. Transfer to carving board; let stand 5 minutes. Slice between ribs to serve.

4 servings.

Preparation time: 30 minutes. Ready to serve: 6 hours.

Per serving: 330 calories, 20.5 g total fat (6.5 g saturated fat), 65 mg cholesterol, 340 mg sodium, 1 g fiber.

DR. PEPPER HAM

COOKING TECHNIQUE: INDIRECT, LOW HEAT WITH A DRIP PAN

Here's a potluck classic, a dish that made the rounds of church socials and family reunions back in the '70s. It's a brilliant way to marinate ham on the grill — and deserves a comeback. Cook only over low heat, so the meat remains moist.

HAM
1 (12-lb.) bone-in smoked ham
20 whole cloves

DR. PEPPER MOP
1 (12-oz.) can Dr. Pepper
¼ cup Dijon mustard
¼ cup frozen orange juice concentrate, thawed
1 tablespoon packed light brown sugar
Vegetable oil for grill grate

1 Score ham, making 5 cuts diagonally through top layer of fat, taking care not to cut into meat. Then make 4 cuts at a 90-degree angle, thereby creating diamond pattern across ham. Press 1 clove into each scoring intersection.

2 Arrange grill for indirect cooking with drip pan under unheated portion of grill grate. Heat grill.

3 **For Mop:** In small bowl, whisk Dr. Pepper, Dijon, orange juice concentrate and brown sugar until sugar dissolves.

4 Brush grill grate with oil. Place ham on gas grill over drip pan, indirectly over low heat; or on charcoal grill over drip pan, but to the side of low-heat coals. Cover; barbecue 2 hours undisturbed. Then cook, basting every 10 minutes with mop, about 1 hour or until browned and meat thermometer inserted in thickest part of ham registers 140°F. Transfer to carving board; let stand 5 minutes.

16 servings.

Preparation time: 20 minutes. Ready to serve: 3 hours.

Per serving: 250 calories, 9 g total fat (3 g saturated fat), 85 mg cholesterol, 1990 mg sodium, 0 g fiber.

WISCONSIN GRILLED SAUSAGES

Grilled sausages are a Wisconsin tradition, particularly at tailgate parties. These sausages are boiled first in a beer and spice mixture, then grilled. If you want, boil them in advance — then store covered in the refrigerator up to one day before grilling.

SAUSAGES

2 (12-oz.) bottles beer

2 cups reduced-sodium chicken broth

2 small onions, cut into quarters

2 teaspoons salt

10 black peppercorns

4 whole cloves

2 lb. pork sausage, such as bratwurst or kielbasa, cut into 6-inch sections

HORSERADISH MUSTARD

¼ cup prepared mustard

2 teaspoons prepared horseradish

½ teaspoon honey

1 **For Sausages:** In large saucepan, bring beer, broth, onions, salt, peppercorns and cloves to a boil over high heat. Add sausage; cover. If using bratwurst or other uncooked sausage, reduce heat to medium; boil 10 minutes. If using kielbasa or other cooked sausage, reduce heat to medium and boil 5 minutes.*

2 **Meanwhile, for Mustard:** In small bowl, whisk mustard, horseradish and honey until blended.

3 Drain sausages; reserve beer mixture. Heat grill for direct cooking.

4 In small saucepan, bring reserved beer mixture to a boil over high heat; boil until reduced by half, about 10 minutes. Strain, discarding onions, peppercorns and cloves.

5 Place sausages on gas grill directly over high heat or on charcoal grill 4 to 6 inches directly over high-heat coals. Grill, mopping with beer glaze and turning occasionally, 8 to 10 minutes or until browned all over. Serve alongside horseradish mustard.

6 servings.

Preparation time: 15 minutes. Ready to serve: 45 minutes.

Per serving: 295 calories, 23 g total fat (8 g saturated fat), 60 mg cholesterol, 1525 mg sodium, 1 g fiber.

TIP *Sausages sometimes pop when boiled, because steam builds up in their casings. If you want, prick each sausage just once before boiling to prevent messy explosions.

STUFFED HOT DOGS

We've all tossed hot dogs on the grate for the kids while the adults' dinner is grilling. But why should the kids have all the fun? These dogs are stuffed with cheese, then wrapped in bacon. Just leave the steaks for the kids!

8   large hot dogs
2   oz. mozzarella cheese, cut into 8 thin, long strips
8   thick slices bacon
8   hot dog buns
2   tablespoons unsalted butter, melted

1 Heat grill for direct cooking.

2 Cut ½-inch-deep slit down each hot dog, taking care not to cut through ends or opposite side. Press mozzarella in slits. Spiral-wrap each hot dog with bacon slice. If desired, secure each end of bacon to hot dog with toothpick; or secure bacon by skewering both ends of all 8 hot dogs with 2 long metal skewers (making a "grate" of dogs).

3 Place stuffed hot dogs on gas grill directly over medium heat or on charcoal grill 4 to 6 inches directly over high-heat coals. Cover; grill, turning once, 6 to 8 minutes or until done.

4 Meanwhile, butter hot dog buns; toast on grill cut-side down 1 minute or until brown. Serve hot dogs in buns with condiments of your choice.

8 servings.

Preparation time: 40 minutes. Ready to serve: 50 minutes.

Per serving: 385 calories, 25 g total fat (10.5 g saturated fat), 45 mg cholesterol, 1020 mg sodium, 1 g fiber.

PINEAPPLE-TERIYAKI PORK TENDERLOINS

Teriyaki marinade is great with pork tenderloins, those small strips of extremely tender meat that run right under the loins. In this marinade version, crushed pineapple and brown sugar function as sweeteners, tweaking the original sauce just a bit.

1   (8-oz.) can crushed pineapple

½   cup soy sauce

¼   cup dry sake or dry sherry

⅓   cup packed light brown sugar

1   tablespoon minced peeled fresh ginger

2   garlic cloves, crushed

2   (1-lb.) pork tenderloins, trimmed of excess fat and silver skin

1   Place pork tenderloins in large resealable plastic bag. In medium bowl, mix pineapple, soy sauce, sake, brown sugar, ginger and garlic until well combined. Reserve one-fourth of the marinade. Pour remaining marinade into bag with tenderloins. Seal bag; shake well to coat. Refrigerate at least 2 hours but no more than 5 hours.

2   Heat grill for direct cooking. Remove tenderloins from marinade; discard marinade.

3   Place tenderloins on gas grill directly over high heat or on charcoal grill 4 to 6 inches directly over high-heat coals. Grill, basting frequently with reserved marinade and turning onto each of its 4 sides, 12 to 15 minutes or until meat thermometer inserted into thickest part of tenderloin registers 160°F for medium (preferred doneness) or 170°F for well-done. Transfer to carving board; let rest 5 minutes. Slice into 1-inch rounds.

4 servings.

Preparation time: 15 minutes. Ready to serve: 2 hours, 40 minutes.

Per serving: 235 calories, 5.5 g total fat (2 g saturated fat), 90 mg cholesterol, 750 mg sodium, 0 g fiber.

EXCITING OPTIONS

Replace the canned crushed pineapple and alter the meat and grilling time for a world of tastes.

Meat	Substitution for the crushed pineapple	Grilling time over high heat after marinating
4 boneless skinless chicken breasts	1 cup apricot nectar	6 minutes per side or until no longer pink in center
24 large shrimp	1 cup pineapple juice	2 minutes per side or until pink throughout
2 lb. top round of beef	1 cup cranberry juice	4 minutes per side

COCONUT-RUBBED PORK SATAY

Satay is the Thai answer to the shish kabob. Thin strips of meat are marinated, skewered and grilled, then served with a fiery dipping sauce, here a coconut/peanut concoction.

PORK

1 small (1½-lb.) boneless pork loin, all exterior fat removed

COCONUT RUB

¼ cup unsweetened coconut flakes (often sold as "coconut chips")

½ teaspoon each packed light brown sugar, ground cinnamon, ground coriander, grated nutmeg

⅛ teaspoon crushed red pepper

3 tablespoons soy sauce

24 to 30 (12-inch) bamboo skewers, soaked in water 20 minutes, then drained

Vegetable oil for grill grate

COCONUT PEANUT DIPPING SAUCE

¼ cup unsweetened coconut milk

¼ cup toasted sesame oil

3 tablespoons peanut butter

2 tablespoons each soy sauce, rice vinegar

1 tablespoon sugar

1 teaspoon chili oil

½ teaspoon freshly ground pepper

1 Cut pork loin in half lengthwise, as if butterflying. Cut each half into ¼-inch-thick slices. Place slices between sheets of parchment or waxed paper; pound with bottom of heavy saucepan to ⅛ inch thick. Place in large bowl.

2 **For Rub:** In spice grinder or coffee grinder, grind coconut, brown sugar, cinnamon, coriander, nutmeg and crushed red pepper. Grind just until uniform (overgrinding will cause coconut fat to produce a paste.) Sprinkle coconut rub and soy sauce into bowl with pork slices; toss to coat. Set aside at room temperature 30 minutes.

3 Heat grill for direct cooking. Place 1 pork slice on each skewer, threading in and out of each side of meat. If desired, wrap exposed ends of skewers in aluminum foil.

4 Brush grill grate with oil. Place skewers on gas grill directly over high heat or on charcoal grill 4 to 6 inches directly over high-heat coals. Grill, turning once, 4 to 5 minutes or until browned and cooked through.

5 Meanwhile, prepare Sauce: In food processor or blender, pulse coconut milk, sesame oil, peanut butter, soy sauce, vinegar, sugar, chili oil and pepper until smooth. Sauce can be prepared ahead. Store, covered, in refrigerator up to 2 days; whisk before serving. Makes about 1 cup.

4 servings.

Preparation time: 1 hour. Ready to serve: 2 hours, 5 minutes.

Per serving: 575 calories, 40 g total fat (13.5 g saturated fat), 110 mg cholesterol, 1410 mg sodium, 2 g fiber.

PULLED PORK

There's nothing like a barbecued pork sandwich. It's the best of Southern barbecuing. Start with a traditional barbecue rub, letting the meat absorb the aromatics. Then barbecue a long time to a very high internal temperature, pull the meat to shards and mix with bottled barbecue sauce for a last simmer on the grill. If you'd like, you can jump it up a level and use one of the sauces in this book, such as the one for Basic Grilled Chicken with Sweet and Spicy Barbecue Sauce *(page 75) or* Beef Ribs with a Plum Barbecue Sauce *(page 38). Admittedly, it's a lot of work — but a lot of reward, too. Serve* Pulled Pork with Grilled Corn Salad *(page 137) or* Grilled Roman Salad *(page 140).*

RUB
- 1 tablespoon packed light brown sugar
- 1 tablespoon chili powder
- 1 tablespoon sweet paprika
- 1 tablespoon salt, preferably sea salt or kosher (coarse) salt
- 1 teaspoon dry mustard
- 1 teaspoon ground cumin
- ½ teaspoon ground cinnamon
- ½ teaspoon freshly ground black pepper
- ¼ teaspoon cayenne pepper

PULLED PORK
- 1 (3½- to 4-lb.) boneless pork shoulder roast
- 1 (8-oz.) bottle barbecue sauce
- 1 cup water
- 4 cups wood chips, soaked in water at least 3 hours or preferably overnight, then drained
- 4 hamburger buns, kaiser rolls or hot dog buns, halved

GARNISH
- 1 bottle pickle relish (optional)

1 **For Rub:** In small bowl, mix brown sugar, chili powder, paprika, salt, mustard, cumin, cinnamon, black pepper and cayenne.

2 **For Pork:** Tie pork shoulder with butcher twine so that it remains closed as an oblong lump, resembling a deflated football.* Massage rub into pork. Cover; refrigerate at least 4 hours, preferably overnight, but no more than 24 hours.

3 Arrange grill for indirect cooking with drip pan under unheated portion of grill grate. Heat grill. If using gas grill, place chips in smoker box; or place chips in small heavy-duty disposable aluminum pan or metal loaf pan, placing pan directly on lava rocks. If using charcoal grill, scatter chips directly on coals or place in disposable pan set directly on coals. Allow chips to begin to smoke, about 10 minutes.

4 Place tied pork shoulder roast on gas grill over drip pan, indirectly at medium heat; or on charcoal grill over drip pan, but to the side of medium-hot coals. Cover; cook 2½ to 3 hours or until meat is charred and falls apart when pulled with fork and meat thermometer inserted halfway into thickest part registers 180°F.

5 Transfer pork to carving board; let rest 5 minutes. Slice off twine; cut meat into small chunks. Shred meat using 2 forks.

6 Place pulled pork in heavy saucepan, preferably cast iron. Add barbecue sauce and water. Heat over medium heat on stove or directly over medium heat on grill grate. Simmer covered 10 minutes or until heated through. Serve on buns. Garnish with pickle relish, if desired.

8 servings.

Preparation time: 30 minutes. Ready to serve: 7 hours.

Per serving: 555 calories, 27 g total fat (9 g saturated fat), 125 mg cholesterol, 1510 mg sodium, 2 g fiber.

TIP *Pay attention to how many strings you've tied around the roast; they can get lost in the crevices of the meat as it cooks. You'll need to know where they are as you pull it apart.

Tandoori Chicken, page 77

POULTRY

While pork or beef may be kings of the grill, chicken still holds a good portion of the day. More chicken is grilled in North America than any other meat. It may not hold the honor of royalty in the barbecue courts, but it certainly holds our hearts. You will use this chapter often — because the recipes are simple, economic and just plain good.

ORANGE GLAZED CHICKEN BREASTS

COOKING TECHNIQUE: DIRECT, MEDIUM HEAT, THEN INDIRECT, MEDIUM HEAT

The sweet glaze seals the juices into chicken breasts as they grill. But don't overcook them! Only leave them on the grill until juices run clear.

1 cup fresh orange juice (about 4 large oranges)

⅓ cup honey, preferably orange-blossom

⅓ cup vinegar

2 teaspoons fresh thyme

1 tablespoon unsalted butter

¼ teaspoon salt

¼ teaspoon freshly ground pepper

15 sprigs thyme, soaked in water 20 minutes, then drained

Vegetable oil for grill grate

4 (12- to 14-oz.) bone-in chicken breasts

1 In small saucepan, heat orange juice, honey, vinegar and 2 teaspoons thyme to a boil. Simmer uncovered over medium-high heat 8 minutes or until reduced and syrupy, whisking occasionally. Whisk in butter, salt and pepper. Glaze can be prepared ahead. Store, covered, in refrigerator up to 2 days; bring to room temperature before using.

2 Divide orange marinade in half, reserving half at room temperature. Heat grill for direct cooking. Place thyme sprigs on lava rocks in gas grill or on ashed briquettes in charcoal grill. Or, place in small disposable aluminum pie pan set directly over heat. Cover grill until thyme begins to smoke.

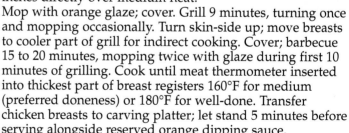

3 Brush grill grate with oil. Place chicken breasts skin-side up on gas grill directly over medium heat or on charcoal grill 4 to 6 inches directly over medium heat. Mop with orange glaze; cover. Grill 9 minutes, turning once and mopping occasionally. Turn skin-side up; move breasts to cooler part of grill for indirect cooking. Cover; barbecue 15 to 20 minutes, mopping twice with glaze during first 10 minutes of grilling. Cook until meat thermometer inserted into thickest part of breast registers 160°F for medium (preferred doneness) or 180°F for well-done. Transfer chicken breasts to carving platter; let stand 5 minutes before serving alongside reserved orange dipping sauce.

4 servings.

Preparation time: 15 minutes. Ready to serve: 50 minutes.

Per serving: 520 calories, 20.5 g total fat (6.5 g saturated fat), 155 mg cholesterol, 275 mg sodium, 0 g fiber.

BARBECUED WHOLE TURKEY WITH A CAJUN RUB

Even if you have to shovel your way to the grill, you still might want to barbecue this moist, tender turkey. But don't wait for Thanksgiving. Turkey is terrific for any get-together!

CAJUN RUB

2   tablespoons salt, preferably sea salt or kosher (coarse) salt

1   tablespoon each sweet paprika, dried parsley

2   teaspoons sugar

1   teaspoon each ground cumin, rubbed sage, celery seed

½   teaspoon freshly ground black pepper

¼   teaspoon each garlic powder, cayenne pepper

TURKEY

1   (12- to 14-lb.) turkey, giblets and pop-up timer removed, rinsed and patted dry*

1   tablespoon vegetable oil, plus additional for grill grate

1   small onion, cut into quarters

1   small green bell pepper, cut into quarters

2   ribs celery, cut into 3-inch segments

1   **For Rub:** In small bowl, combine salt, paprika, parsley, sugar, cumin, sage, celery seed, black pepper, garlic powder and cayenne.

2   **For Turkey:** Oil turkey skin with 1 tablespoon oil. Massage cajun rub onto turkey skin. If desired, massage 1 teaspoon rub under skin directly onto breast meat. Stuff large cavity with onion, bell pepper and celery. Tie legs together with butcher twine to protect breast; tie wings to side of bird as well. Set aside at room temperature while grill heats.

3   Arrange grill for indirect cooking with drip pan under unheated portion of grill grate. Heat grill. Place turkey on gas grill over drip pan, indirectly over medium heat; or on charcoal grill over drip pan, but to the side of medium-hot coals. Cover; barbecue about 2½ hours or until meat thermometer inserted into the thickest part of the thigh registers 180°F and into thickest part of breast registers 170°F. Transfer to carving board; let rest 5 minutes before carving.

10 to 12 servings.

Preparation time: 20 minutes. Ready to serve: 2 hours, 55 minutes.

Per serving: 330 calories, 12 g total fat (3.5 g saturated fat), 140 mg cholesterol, 1535 mg sodium, 0.5 g fiber.

TIP *You'll want to measure the distance from the grill grate to the lid before you start this recipe. Some gas grills, particularly older models, may not be large enough to handle a whole turkey. If you have hanging baskets in your lid, remove them before barbecuing the bird.

TAPENADE-MARINATED CHICKEN GRILLED UNDER A BRICK

This is a classic Italian technique, a favorite in trattoria and lunch counters across that country. Because the thighs are boneless, they cook in minutes with bricks weighing them down and sealing in the juices. Use grilling mitts to move the bricks, because they get very hot.

⅔	cup tapenade*
¼	cup olive oil
2	tablespoons chopped fresh oregano
1	garlic clove, crushed
16	(3- to 4-oz.) boneless skinless chicken thighs
6 to 8	bricks, wrapped tightly but smoothly in aluminum foil

1 In large bowl, mix tapenade, olive oil, oregano and garlic. Add thighs; toss to coat. Cover; refrigerate at least 2 hours but no more than 24 hours.

2 Heat grill for direct cooking. Remove thighs from refrigerator while grill heats. Do not drain thighs.

3 Place wrapped bricks in single layer on gas grill directly over high heat or on charcoal grill 4 to 6 inches directly over high-heat coals. Cover; heat bricks 10 minutes.

4 Using grilling mitts, remove 1 brick and place 2 to 3 thighs (with marinade adhering) in its place on grill directly over high heat. Top with removed, hot brick. Repeat with remaining bricks and thighs. Discard any remaining marinade. Cover; grill 5 to 8 minutes or until juices run clear. Remove bricks; turn thighs. Cook 1 minute to crisp. Serve immediately.

8 servings.

Preparation time: 10 minutes. Ready to serve: 2 hours, 20 minutes.

Per serving: 330 calories, 19.5 g total fat (4.5 g saturated fat), 115 mg cholesterol, 330 mg sodium, 0.5 g fiber.

TIP *Tapenade is a salty olive paste, often served as an appetizer with crackers. It's found with the other condiments in gourmet markets, either "fresh" in the refrigerator case or bottled in the condiment section.

BUFFALO CHICKEN WINGS WITH A BLUE CHEESE DIP

COOKING TECHNIQUE: DIRECT, MEDIUM HEAT

Buffalo wings are usually deep-fried, but they're excellent hot off the grill, first marinated in a fiery butter sauce, then served with their traditional blue cheese dipping sauce.

BLUE CHEESE DIP

1½ cups mayonnaise (regular, low-fat or nonfat)

½ cup sour cream (regular, low-fat or nonfat)

½ cup (2 oz.) crumbled blue cheese, such as Danish Blue or Gorgonzola

2 tablespoons minced red onion

2 tablespoons lemon juice

1 teaspoon salt

½ teaspoon garlic powder

½ teaspoon freshly ground pepper

WINGS

½ cup (1 stick) unsalted butter, melted, cooled

½ cup or to taste hot pepper sauce, such as Texas Pete's or Tiger Sauce

1 tablespoon Worcestershire sauce

2 teaspoons packed light brown sugar

24 chicken wings, tips removed, tiny drumsticks divided from winglets

1 **For Dip:** In small bowl, mix together mayonnaise, sour cream, blue cheese, red onion, lemon juice, salt, garlic powder and pepper until uniform. Dip can be prepared in advance. Store, covered, in refrigerator up to 2 days; bring to room temperature before serving.

2 **For Wings:** In medium bowl, whisk together butter, hot pepper sauce, Worcestershire and brown sugar. Pour ½ cup hot pepper marinade into large bowl; reserve remainder at room temperature. Add chicken wings to marinade in bowl. Toss to coat; marinate 30 minutes at room temperature.

3 Heat grill for direct cooking.

4 Place chicken wings on gas grill directly over medium heat or on charcoal grill 4 to 6 inches directly over medium coals. Grill, turning once, 6 to 8 minutes or until golden. (If your grill grate is small, you may need to grill wings in batches.)

5 Transfer wings to large bowl; toss with reserved marinade. Serve with dip.

10 to 12 appetizer servings.

Preparation time: 25 minutes. Ready to serve: 1 hour, 10 minutes.

Per serving: 595 calories, 54.5 g total fat (15.5 g saturated fat), 120 mg cholesterol, 825 mg sodium, 0 g fiber.

BASIC GRILLED CHICKEN WITH A SWEET AND SPICY BARBECUE SAUCE

COOKING TECHNIQUE: DIRECT, MEDIUM HEAT

Here's the classic: a tangy, tomato-based barbecue sauce, mopped onto chicken as it grills. If you want, make a double batch of the sauce, freeze what you don't need and save it for your next grilling extravaganza. Although it's designed to match the taste of chicken, this sauce also goes well with ribs, veggies and even brisket.

BARBECUE SAUCE

1	(6-oz.) can tomato paste
⅔	cup water
½	cup packed dark brown sugar
¼	cup unsulphured dark molasses
¼	cup light corn syrup
¼	cup cider vinegar
1	tablespoon Worcestershire sauce
1½	teaspoons chili powder
1	teaspoon garlic powder
1	teaspoon onion powder
1	teaspoon salt
1	teaspoon freshly ground black pepper
¼	teaspoon cayenne pepper
½	teaspoon liquid smoke seasoning (optional)

CHICKEN

Vegetable oil for grill grate
1   (4- to 5-lb.) chicken, cut into 8 or 9 pieces

1 **For Sauce:** In medium saucepan, heat tomato paste, water, brown sugar, molasses, corn syrup, vinegar, Worcestershire, chili powder, garlic powder, onion powder, salt, black pepper, cayenne and liquid smoke, if using, to a simmer over medium heat. Reduce heat to low; simmer uncovered 10 minutes, stirring frequently. Barbecue sauce can also be made on grill: Place heavy-duty saucepan on grill grate directly over medium heat. Sauce can be prepared ahead. Store, covered, in refrigerator up to 4 days.

2 Heat grill for direct cooking.

3 **For Chicken:** Brush grill grate with oil. Place chicken skin-side down on gas grill directly over medium heat or on charcoal grill 4 to 6 inches directly over medium-hot coals. Cover; grill 16 to 18 minutes, turning once and mopping frequently with barbecue sauce. Breasts, wings and back will be done first. A meat thermometer inserted into thickest part of breast should register 160°F for medium (preferred doneness) or 170°F for well-done. Move breasts, wings and back to cool part of grate. Cover; grill thighs and legs 5 to 10 minutes to reach 160°F for medium or 180°F for well-done. Mop with any remaining sauce; transfer to carving board. Let stand 5 minutes.

6 servings.

Preparation time: 15 minutes. Ready to serve: 55 minutes.

Per serving: 380 calories, 15 g total fat (4.5 g saturated fat), 110 mg cholesterol, 440 mg sodium, 1 g fiber.

TANDOORI CHICKEN

Since most of us don't have a tandoori oven, a barbecue is a good stand-in. This simple dish is best served with Na'an (an Indian flatbread, page 154) or perhaps lefse or lavash, along with mango chutney, tomatoes and cucumber mint raita.

MARINADE

2   cups plain yogurt (regular or low-fat)
2   tablespoons lemon juice
1   tablespoon chili powder
2   teaspoons each salt, ground ginger, ground coriander
½   teaspoon each garlic powder, freshly ground pepper

CHICKEN

1   (4-lb.) chicken, cut into 8 or 9 pieces
    Vegetable oil for grill grate
1   large onion, sliced into ½-inch-thick rings
2   lemons, cut into wedges

CUCUMBER MINT RAITA

1   large cucumber, peeled, seeded and finely chopped
3   cups plain yogurt (regular, low-fat or nonfat)
1   tablespoon minced fresh mint
½   teaspoon salt
    Dash cayenne pepper (optional)

1 **For Marinade:** In large bowl, whisk all ingredients until smooth. Divide chicken breast pieces in half (making 4 pieces of breast meat). Add chicken pieces to yogurt mixture; toss to coat. Cover; refrigerate at least 2 hours but no more than 6 hours.

2 Heat grill for direct cooking. Let chicken and marinade stand at room temperature while grill heats.

3 **For Chicken:** Remove chicken from marinade, shaking off excess but leaving a thin coating; discard marinade. Brush grill grate with oil. Place chicken legs and thighs skin-side down on gas grill directly over high heat or on charcoal grill 4 to 6 inches directly over high-heat coals. Cover; grill 3 minutes. Add breast pieces skin-side down. Cover; grill all pieces, turning once, 12 to 15 minutes or until juices run clear and meat thermometer inserted into thickest part of thigh registers 160°F for medium or 180°F for well-done. Transfer chicken to platter; tent with foil to keep warm.

4 Brush grill grate with oil again. Add onion slices over direct high heat. Cook 2 minutes or until browned. Turn; add lemon wedges alongside, rind-side down. Cook 2 minutes or until onions are brown. Transfer to platter with chicken.

5 Meanwhile, for cucumber mint raita: In medium bowl, stir together all ingredients until well combined. (Store, covered, in refrigerator up to 2 days. Before serving, remix to incorporate any separation.)

4 servings.

Preparation time: 25 minutes. Ready to serve: 2 hours, 50 minutes.

Per serving: 1365 calories, 48.5 g total fat (18 g saturated fat), 265 mg cholesterol, 2410 mg sodium, 7 g fiber.

CHICKEN SITTING ON A BEER CAN

It's a startling sight: a chicken sitting bolt upright on a beer can on your grill grate! But you'll be delighted with the taste. The beer steams the chicken from the inside while the outside becomes crisp and delicious. From appearance to taste, Chicken Sitting on a Beer Can *will make your next barbecue memorable.*

2 teaspoons salt, preferably sea salt or kosher (coarse) salt

1 teaspoon each celery seed, dried lemon peel

½ teaspoon each rubbed sage, garlic powder, onion powder, freshly ground pepper

1 (4- to 5-lb.) whole chicken, giblets removed, rinsed and patted dry

1 (12- or 16-oz.) tall can beer

1 In small bowl, mix salt, celery seed, lemon peel, sage, garlic powder, onion powder and pepper. Rub onto chicken, massaging into skin. If desired, rub ½ teaspoon spice mixture under breast skin, directly onto breast meat.

2 Arrange grill for indirect cooking with drip pan under unheated portion of grill grate. Heat grill.

3 Open beer; discard half of beer. Use church-key can opener to create second opening in can's lid, opposite pull-top. In medium saucepan, bring 4 cups water to a boil. Remove from heat; place beer can in hot water. Let stand 5 minutes or until beer is warmed. Using grilling gloves or hot pad, place can on work surface. Slip chicken over can so can fits about halfway into large cavity.

4 Transfer chicken and beer can to grill grate. On gas grill, over drip pan, indirectly over medium heat. Or, on charcoal grill, over drip pan but to the side of medium-hot coals. Use can and chicken's legs to balance bird upright on grate. Cover; cook 1¼ to 1½ hours or until meat thermometer inserted into thickest part of thigh registers 160°F for medium (preferred doneness) or 180°F for well-done. Using heavy tongs, spatulas and/or grilling gloves, transfer chicken and can to carving board; let stand 10 minutes. Remove and discard can. Carve chicken for serving.

6 servings.

Preparation time: 15 minutes. Ready to serve: 1 hour, 55 minutes.

Per serving: 295 calories, 15.5 g total fat (4.5 g saturated fat), 110 mg cholesterol, 875 mg sodium, 0 g fiber.

SAGE PESTO TURKEY LONDON BROIL

COOKING TECHNIQUE: DIRECT, MEDIUM HEAT

Boneless turkey breast, sliced into thin strips, marinated in sage pesto and then grilled — think of it as a new take on London Broil! The sage pesto marinade can also be made on its own and served as a sauce with ziti or other tubular pasta, cooked according to the package instructions. Sage pesto also makes a nice accompaniment to Tequila-Brined Pork Chops *(page 56), or a great accent to* Tapenade-Marinated Chicken Grilled Under a Brick *(page 72).*

SAGE PESTO

1   cup packed fresh Italian parsley

¼   cup tightly packed fresh sage

2   tablespoons toasted pine nuts*

2   tablespoons freshly grated Parmesan cheese

3   garlic cloves, minced

1   teaspoon salt

½   teaspoon freshly ground pepper

1   cup olive oil, plus additional for grill grate

TURKEY

1   (2-lb.) boneless turkey breast

1   **For Pesto:** Place parsley, sage, pine nuts, Parmesan, garlic, salt and pepper in blender or food processor. Pour 1 cup olive oil over top; pulse to blend, scraping down sides of container as necessary. Process 1 minute or until pureed.

2   **For Turkey:** Slice turkey breast into 12 equal slices on the bias by placing knife at a 45-degree angle to cutting surface and making long, even strokes through meat. Place slices in large bowl; toss with pesto. Set aside to marinate 30 minutes.

3   Heat grill for direct cooking.

4   Brush grill grate with oil. Place turkey slices (with pesto adhering) on gas grill directly over medium heat or on charcoal grill 4 to 6 inches directly over medium coals. Grill, turning once, 6 to 7 minutes or until lightly browned.

6 servings.

Preparation time: 20 minutes. Ready to serve: 1 hour.

Per serving: 585 calories, 50 g total fat (8.5 g saturated fat), 90 mg cholesterol, 510 mg sodium, 0.5 g fiber.

TIP *To toast pine nuts, place on baking sheet; bake at 350°F for 6 minutes or until golden, stirring occasionally.

GRILLED CHICKEN SANDWICHES

COOKING TECHNIQUE: DIRECT, HIGH HEAT

Boneless skinless chicken breasts dry out on the grill, often shrinking into hockey-puck results. So brine them first — that way, they're plump and moist right off the grate.

1	small onion, sliced
3	bay leaves
4	(6- to 8-oz.) boneless skinless chicken breasts
3	cups water
¼	cup salt, preferably sea salt or kosher (coarse) salt
2	tablespoons honey
10	black peppercorns, crushed
	Vegetable oil for grill grate
1	beefsteak tomato, cut into 4 slices
1	small red onion, thickly sliced
8	large thick-cut slices white or country white bread
1	large ripe avocado, peeled, pitted and sliced
1	cup bean, garlic or radish sprouts
	Mayonnaise, mustard or bottled vinaigrette to taste, for garnish

1 Place onion and bay leaves in medium baking dish. Lay chicken breasts on top. In medium bowl, whisk water and salt until salt dissolves; whisk in honey and peppercorns. Pour over chicken breasts. Cover; refrigerate at least 2 hours but no more than 6 hours, turning breasts occasionally without disturbing onions.

2 Heat grill for direct cooking. Remove chicken from marinade; discard marinade. Pat chicken dry with paper towels. Let stand at room temperature while grill heats.

3 Brush grill grate with oil. Place breasts on gas grill directly over high heat or on charcoal grill 4 to 6 inches directly over high-heat coals. Grill, turning once, 11 to 13 minutes or until meat thermometer inserted into thickest part of breast registers 160°F for medium (preferred doneness) or 180°F for well-done. Transfer to carving board; let rest 5 minutes. Maintain grill temperature.

4 Brush grill grate with oil again. Place tomato and red onion slices over high heat; grill, turning once, 3 minutes or until browned and soft. Transfer to carving board; set aside.

5 Place bread slices on grill over high heat. Toast, turning once, 1 minute or until brown. Transfer to carving board. Slice chicken into strips, if desired. Assemble sandwiches on bread with chicken strips, tomato slices, red onion slices, sliced avocado, sprouts and mayonnaise, mustard or bottled vinaigrette.

4 servings.

Preparation time: 25 minutes. Ready to serve: 2 hours, 45 minutes.

Per serving: 510 calories, 18.5 g total fat (3.5 g saturated fat), 95 mg cholesterol, 2190 mg sodium, 5.5 g fiber.

Lamb Shish Kabobs, page 91

LAMB

For much of the world, particularly the Middle East and Central Asia, grilling means lamb. No wonder — it's fatty enough to stand up to long cooking, and plentiful in countries where grazing cattle would be an impossibility. Unfortunately, lamb has gotten a bad reputation in the United States. Some say it's gamey; others, tough. But if cooked properly, lamb mellows on the grill. It simply needs to be marinated in the right blend of spices, usually those redolent of Greece, Turkey or the Middle East.

RACK OF LAMB WITH A GREMOLATA RUB

Rack of lamb is an elegant dinner for a no-fuss world. This rub is a version of the classic gremolata, a spice mixture from southern Italy, the classic flavoring for osso buco — but it's redolent of foods served across the heat-splashed Mediterranean.

GREMOLATA RUB

2 tablespoons chopped fresh parsley

2 tablespoons chopped fresh oregano

2 tablespoons chopped fresh rosemary

1 tablespoon grated lemon peel

1 teaspoon chopped fresh mint

1 teaspoon salt

½ teaspoon freshly ground pepper

LAMB

3 tablespoons olive oil, plus additional for grill grate

3 (6-bone, ¾-lb.) racks of lamb, trimmed of all visible fat*

1 For Rub: In small bowl, mix parsley, oregano, rosemary, lemon peel, mint, salt and pepper.

2 For Lamb: Rub 1 tablespoon oil into meat of each rack. Press one-third of rub into meat side of each rack. (The meat side is the one that's "up" when the bones curve down.)

3 Arrange grill for indirect cooking with drip pan under unheated portion of grill grate. Heat grill.

4 Brush grill grate with oil. Place racks herb-side up on gas grill over drip pan, indirectly over high heat; or on charcoal grill over drip pan, but to the side of high-heat coals. Cover; barbecue 25 to 30 minutes or until meat thermometer inserted halfway into meat (but missing bones) registers 145°F for medium-rare (preferred doneness) or 160°F for medium. During prolonged grilling, the bones, especially if frenched, may burn. If so, place thin sheet of aluminum foil between bones and grill grate. Transfer to carving board; let rest 2 minutes. Carve between chops to serve.

4 servings.

Preparation time: 25 minutes. Ready to serve: 45 minutes.

Per serving: 255 calories, 19.5 g total fat (4.5 g saturated fat), 60 mg cholesterol, 640 mg sodium, 0.5 g fiber.

TIP *If possible, have your butcher "french" the racks — he'll trim the fat off of and from between the bones, making a better presentation for the final dish. But don't have your butcher cut the chops apart. Roast them as a whole rack, then slice before serving.

CURRIED LAMB KABOBS

This is the traditional way lamb kabobs are made in Turkey — surprisingly, with ground lamb, which is formed around the skewer, like a long sausage.

1   lb. ground lamb

½   small onion, minced

1   garlic clove, minced

1   tablespoon minced peeled fresh ginger

1   tablespoon minced fresh cilantro

1   teaspoon curry powder*

½   teaspoon salt

4   metal skewers or 4 (12-inch) bamboo skewers, soaked in water 20 minutes, then drained

1   tablespoon plus 1 teaspoon olive oil, plus additional for grill grate

1 In medium bowl, mix ground lamb, onion, garlic, ginger, cilantro, curry powder and salt until uniform. Lamb mixture can be prepared ahead. Store, covered, in refrigerator up to 1 day; bring to room temperature before using.

2 Heat grill for direct cooking. Form one-fourth lamb mixture around each skewer; use your hands to shape it into even, sausage-like loaf running down skewer. Brush each kabob with 1 teaspoon olive oil. If using bamboo skewers, wrap ends in aluminum foil to prevent burning.

3 Brush grill grate with oil. Place skewers on gas grill directly over high heat or on charcoal grill directly over high-heat coals. Cover; grill, turning once, about 12 minutes or until meat is browned throughout and firm. Transfer to carving board; let stand 5 minutes before pulling skewers from kabobs.

4 servings.

Preparation time: 15 minutes. Ready to serve: 30 minutes.

Per serving: 265 calories, 20 g total fat (7 g saturated fat), 70 mg cholesterol, 345 mg sodium, 0.5 g fiber.

TIP *Curry powder is not a single spice, nor even a set blend. It's a blend that usually includes fenugreek, ginger and other aromatics, often cut with turmeric. Because of chemical reactions among the spices, curry powder goes stale quickly; store curry powder in refrigerator no more than two months. You could also use madras curry powder for this recipe, a spicy blend cut with cayenne pepper rather than turmeric.

STUFFED LEG OF LAMB

This leg of lamb is stuffed with olives, cheese and caponata (a classic Italian appetizer of eggplant, tomato and capers). For this dish, splurge on good, imported Parmesan cheese, always stamped "Parmigiano-Reggiano" on the rind. Don't use "grated Parmesan" in cans, which is made mostly from oil.

1   (2½- lb.) half boneless leg of lamb, preferably sirloin end, butterflied

1   (5-oz.) jar caponata or Italian eggplant appetizer

2   tablespoons oil-cured ripe olives, pitted

2   oz. Parmesan cheese, shaved into paper-thin strips

1   tablespoon olive oil, plus additional for grill grate

½   teaspoon salt, preferably sea salt or kosher (coarse) salt

½   teaspoon freshly ground pepper

1 Lay leg of lamb cut-side up on work surface. Spread caponata over meat, leaving ½-inch border on all sides. Dot with olives; lay Parmesan on top. Roll leg up the long way, jelly-roll fashion; make firm, but not tight, roll to prevent caponata from leaking. Tie roll in 3 or 4 places to close — not tightly, but just so it holds its shape as it roasts. Rub any caponata that comes out onto outside of meat along with olive oil, salt and pepper. Place rolled leg in large baking dish. Cover; refrigerate at least 4 hours but no more than 12 hours.

2 Heat grill for direct cooking. Let stuffed leg stand at room temperature while grill heats.

3 Brush grill grate with oil. Place stuffed leg on gas grill directly over medium heat or on charcoal grill 4 to 6 inches directly over medium-hot coals. Grill, turning occasionally, about 50 minutes or until golden on all sides and meat thermometer inserted into meat (but not stuffing) registers 160°F for medium or 170°F for well-done. Transfer to carving board; let rest 5 minutes.

6 servings.

Preparation time: 4 hours, 40 minutes. Ready to serve: 5 hours, 30 minutes.

Per serving: 375 calories, 20 g total fat (7 g saturated fat), 140 mg cholesterol, 520 mg sodium, 0.5 g fiber.

LAMB SHISH KABOBS

No doubt about it, shish kabobs are both a Turkish delicacy and an American backyard favorite. Here, avoid lamb labeled "stew meat," for it is tough.

2 teaspoons dried dill

2 teaspoons salt

1½ teaspoons each dried oregano, dried rosemary

1 teaspoon each fennel seeds, freshly ground pepper

1 bay leaf

1½ lb. boneless lamb loin, leg or shoulder, cut into 1½-inch cubes (about 24 pieces)

3 garlic cloves, minced

6 tablespoons olive oil, plus additional for grill grate

6 long metal skewers or 6 (12-inch) bamboo skewers, soaked in water 20 minutes, then drained

2 small green bell peppers, cut into sixths

2 small red onions, cut into sixths

1 tablespoon lemon juice

1 In spice grinder or coffee grinder, grind dill, salt, oregano, rosemary, fennel seeds, pepper and bay leaf until powdery. In large bowl, toss spice mixture, lamb, garlic and 3 tablespoons of the olive oil to coat. Cover; refrigerate at least 4 hours but no more than 24 hours.

2 Heat grill for direct cooking. Skewer lamb, bell peppers and red onions, using 4 pieces of meat and 2 pieces each of bell pepper and red onion on each skewer, alternating meat and vegetables. In small bowl, whisk 3 tablespoons of the olive oil and lemon juice.

3 Brush grill grate with olive oil. Place skewers on gas grill directly over high heat or on charcoal grill 4 to 6 inches directly over high-heat coals.* Grill, brushing occasionally with olive oil mixture, 12 to 15 minutes or until brown and meat thermometer inserted into lamb cube registers 160°F for medium or 170°F for well-done. Transfer to carving board; let rest 5 minutes before unspearing.

6 servings.

Preparation time: 4 hours, 30 minutes. Ready to serve: 4 hours, 45 minutes.

Per serving: 310 calories, 21.5 g total fat (4.5 g saturated fat), 80 mg cholesterol, 840 mg sodium, 1 g fiber.

TIP *If using metal skewers, be careful — they become hot on a superheated grill. Turn skewers with metal tongs or while wearing grilling gloves. Place skewers on grill the long way; otherwise, the lid will close on them and tilt the meat up off the grate.

LAMB SHOULDER CHOPS WITH AN ONION MARINADE

This is the classic way to barbecue lamb across much of Central Asia. Serve this unusual but tasty dish with an aromatic rice, such as Texmati, or even that American favorite, wild rice.

ONION MARINADE

¼ teaspoon saffron threads

2 teaspoons hot water

2 medium red onions

2 red bell peppers, cored, seeded

2 teaspoons salt

1 teaspoon sweet paprika

1 teaspoon crushed red pepper

½ teaspoon ground cumin

CHOPS

8 (7- to 9- oz.) lamb shoulder chops

Vegetable oil for grill grate

1 **For Marinade:** Crumble saffron threads into small bowl; add hot water. Steep 5 minutes. Meanwhile, grate red onions and bell peppers using fine holes of box grater. Alternately, pulse in food processor until consistency of applesauce. Transfer grated onions and peppers to fine-mesh sieve or colander lined with cheesecloth; place over large bowl to catch drippings. Let drain 5 minutes; gently press mixture with back of wooden spoon to release as much liquid as possible. Discard onion and pepper pulp. Stir saffron mixture, salt, paprika, crushed red pepper and cumin into onion/pepper liquid.

2 **For Chops:** Place chops in large baking dish; alternately, place in large resealable plastic bag. Pour marinade over chops; cover or seal. Refrigerate at least 2 hours but no more than 4 hours.

3 Heat grill for direct cooking. Let chops and marinade come to room temperature while grill heats.

4 Drain chops; discard marinade. Brush grill grate with oil. Place chops on gas grill directly over high heat or on charcoal grill 4 to 6 inches over high-heat coals. Grill, turning once, 7 to 9 minutes or until browned and meat thermometer inserted into chop registers 145°F for medium-rare or 160°F for medium. Transfer to plates to serve.

4 servings.

Preparation time: 2 hours, 30 minutes. Ready to serve: 2 hours, 40 minutes.

Per serving: 375 calories, 16.5 g total fat (6 g saturated fat), 165 mg cholesterol, 420 mg sodium, 0.5 g fiber.

GRILLED LEG OF LAMB WITH A BASIL MINT PESTO MARINADE

Look no further for a classic leg of lamb on (or off) the grate. This pesto, spiked with walnuts, slowly infuses the boneless, butterflied meat as it cooks. For a taste of the Mediterranean, serve this hearty meal with roasted tomato soup (see Sidebar, page 141) and Grilled Polenta *(page 145).*

BASIL MINT PESTO

2   cups packed fresh basil
1   cup olive oil, plus additional for grill grate
½   cup chopped toasted walnuts*
¼   cup packed fresh mint
2   tablespoons freshly grated Parmesan cheese
1   tablespoon salt
2   teaspoons freshly ground pepper
4   garlic cloves, cut into quarters

LAMB

1   (4-lb.) boneless leg of lamb, butterflied

1   For Pesto: In blender or food processor, pulse basil, olive oil, walnuts, mint, Parmesan, salt, pepper and garlic to blend, scraping down sides of bowl as necessary. Process about 1 minute or until pureed.

2   For Lamb: Place lamb leg in large baking dish or large resealable plastic bag. Pour pesto over lamb. If using baking dish, turn to coat and cover; if using plastic bag, seal and shake well. Refrigerate at least 4 hours but no more than 24 hours.

3   Heat grill for direct cooking. Allow lamb and pesto to stand at room temperature while grill heats.

4   Brush grill grate with oil. Remove lamb from marinade, preserving as much pesto on meat as possible. Place flat on grill directly over medium heat or on charcoal grill 4 to 6 inches directly over medium-hot coals. Cover; grill, turning once, 12 to 14 minutes or until browned and meat thermometer inserted into thickest part of meat registers 145°F for medium-rare or 160°F for medium (preferred doneness). Reduce grill heat to low if lamb starts to blacken. Transfer to carving board; let rest 5 minutes. Slice on the bias by placing knife at a 45-degree angle to carving board; make long slices through meat.

8 to 10 servings.

Preparation time: 4 hours, 25 minutes. Ready to serve: 4 hours, 45 minutes.

Per serving: 500 calories, 32 g total fat (7.5 g saturated fat), 155 mg cholesterol, 570 mg sodium, 0.5 g fiber.

TIP *To toast walnuts, place in medium skillet over low heat; cook until lightly browned and fragrant, about 4 minutes, tossing frequently.

SOUVLAKI

All across Manhattan, people line up for Souvlaki *at stands, which are simply grills set up on street corners. You can make this Manhattan lunch favorite for your next backyard barbecue. Tell your guests you got the idea from a guy at the corner of 48th and 6th.*

½ cup olive oil

¼ cup lemon juice

4 garlic cloves, crushed

2 teaspoons chopped fresh oregano

1½ teaspoons salt

½ teaspoon freshly ground pepper

1½ lb. lamb loin, cut into ¾-inch cubes

2 cups yogurt (regular, low-fat or nonfat)

1 small cucumber, peeled, seeded and shredded

2 teaspoons chopped fresh dill

4 metal skewers or 4 (12-inch) bamboo skewers, soaked in water 20 minutes, then drained

6 pita pockets

Shredded lettuce, diced tomatoes and thinly sliced red onions, for garnish

1 In large bowl, whisk olive oil, lemon juice, 2 of the garlic cloves, oregano, 1 teaspoon of the salt and pepper until well combined. Add lamb cubes; toss to coat. Cover; refrigerate at least 1 hour but no more than 3 hours.

2 Heat grill for direct cooking. Bring lamb and its marinade back to room temperature while grill heats.

3 Meanwhile, in medium bowl, mix yogurt, cucumber, dill, remaining 2 garlic cloves and remaining ½ teaspoon salt. Dressing can be made in advance — refrigerate, covered, up to 3 days.

4 Thread marinated lamb cubes onto skewers. (Do not blot lamb dry.) Fit as many cubes as you please on skewers without crowding — this is only to aid grilling, not for presentation. Place lamb skewers on gas grill directly over high heat or on charcoal grill 4 to 6 inches directly over high-heat coals. Cover; grill, turning once, about 8 minutes or until meat thermometer inserted in middle cube on 1 skewer registers 160°F for medium or 170°F for well-done.

5 Build Souvlaki by placing grilled lamb cubes and dressing in pita pockets; top with lettuce, tomato and red onion, as desired.

6 servings.

Preparation time: 1 hour, 30 minutes. Ready to serve: 1 hour, 40 minutes.

Per serving: 450 calories, 20.5 g total fat (6 g saturated fat), 90 mg cholesterol, 735 mg sodium, 2 g fiber.

Apricot Grilled Pheasant with a Grilled Apricot Relish, page 102

GAME

Game is a civilized pleasure. Quail, pheasant, venison, elk — on the grill, they may be primal, yet they're ever so sophisticated. For some enthusiasts, game is the grail of the grill, the food that best captures the grate's smoky flavors. Because game meat is invariably lean, it is a little more temperamental than beef or chicken. You have to marinate elk longer, fat a wild turkey with bacon, tenderize a pheasant. But the rewards match the efforts. Try a few of these recipes and you'll become an enthusiast too.

QUAIL WITH A POMEGRANATE ALMOND MARINADE

COOKING TECHNIQUE: DIRECT, HIGH HEAT

With a simple marinade, you can turn these small game birds into five-star delights. If you get farm-raised quail, the meat is much milder than wild quail — but not as adventuresome either. If you have wild birds, let them marinate four to six hours in the sour pomegranate sauce.

POMEGRANATE ALMOND MARINADE

½ cup pomegranate molasses*

¼ cup almond oil

¼ cup water

1 tablespoon minced fresh mint

1 tablespoon packed light brown sugar

1 teaspoon salt

½ teaspoon freshly ground pepper

QUAIL

4 (4- to 4½-oz.) quail, cleaned, split down the back and opened flat**

1 **For Marinade:** In large bowl, whisk pomegranate molasses, almond oil, water, mint, brown sugar, salt and pepper until blended. Add quail; toss to coat. Cover; refrigerate at least 2 hours but no more than 6 hours.

2 Heat grill for direct cooking. Drain quail; reserve marinade. Let stand at room temperature while grill heats.

3 **For Quail:** Place quail skin-side up on gas grill directly over high heat or on charcoal grill 4 to 6 inches directly over high-heat coals. Cover; grill, brushing occasionally with marinade, 5 minutes or until lightly browned. Flip with spatula or tongs; move quail to cooler section of grate. Mop with marinade; cover. Cook 2 minutes or until browned.

4 servings.

Preparation time: 2 hours, 30 minutes. Ready to serve: 2 hours, 40 minutes.

Per serving: 200 calories, 11 g total fat (2.5 g saturated fat), 55 mg cholesterol, 205 mg sodium, 0 g fiber.

TIP *Pomegranate molasses is a Lebanese delicacy: boiled-down, highly concentrated pomegranate juice. If you can't find it, you can substitute frozen cranberry juice concentrate, thawed but not diluted with water.

TIP **Quail are best cooked quickly, so opening them out flat allows the most meat to come in contact with the heat for the least amount of time. To open a bird, place the quail breast-side up on work surface. Insert sharp knife into body cavity and press down, right through the backbone, with steady, firm pressure.

MOROCCAN-RUBBED SQUABS

COOKING TECHNIQUE: INDIRECT, MEDIUM HEAT WITH A DRIP PAN

When done, a squab's juices will still run pink, a no-no for chicken but just right for these wild fowl, whose dark meat is stronger than pheasant or quail.

SQUABS

- 2 tablespoons unsalted butter
- ¼ cup slivered almonds
- 4 (1-lb.) squabs, cleaned but livers reserved
- 1 cup reduced-sodium chicken broth
- ¾ cup couscous (½ of a 10-oz. box)
- 1 tablespoon salt
- ½ teaspoon freshly ground pepper
- ¼ cup currants or chopped raisins

MOROCCAN RUB

- 2 teaspoons ground cumin
- 2 teaspoons ground turmeric
- 1 teaspoon ground cinnamon
- 1 teaspoon ground ginger
- ½ teaspoon dry mustard
- ¼ cup almond oil or vegetable oil, plus additional for grill grate and basting birds

1 **For Squabs:** In medium saucepan, melt butter over medium heat. Add almonds; sauté 2 minutes or until fragrant and brown. Meanwhile, finely chop squab livers. Add to saucepan with almonds. Cook 1 minute, stirring constantly. Remove from heat; transfer to medium bowl to cool.

2 In medium saucepan, bring broth to a simmer over medium heat. Stir in couscous, 1 teaspoon of the salt and pepper. Cover; remove from heat. Let stand 5 minutes. Stir into almond mixture along with currants. Alternately, almonds, squabs and couscous can be made directly on grill: Use heavy-duty medium saucepans placed on grill grate directly over medium heat.

3 Stuff couscous mixture into squabs' body cavities. Pat mixture down to fill cavity, but not until firm. Truss birds by wrapping butcher twine around legs to seal in stuffing. Brush off any couscous stuffing adhering to skin.

4 **For Rub:** In small bowl, mix cumin, remaining 2 teaspoons salt, turmeric, cinnamon, ginger and mustard until uniform; stir in oil until smooth. Massage one-fourth rub onto skin of each squab, coating skin entirely.

5 Arrange grill for indirect cooking with drip pan under unheated portion of grill grate. Heat grill. Brush grill grate with oil. Place squabs breast-side up on gas grill over drip pan, indirectly over medium heat; or on charcoal grill over drip pan, but to the side of medium-hot coals. Cover; grill 30 minutes, brushing breasts once or twice with additional oil. Turn birds breast-side down on grill rack; grill over indirect, medium heat about 20 minutes or until lightly browned and until meat thermometer inserted into thickest part of thigh registers 160°F for medium or 175°F for well done (at medium, the preferred doneness, meat is pink). Transfer to carving board; let stand 5 minutes before removing twine.

4 servings.

Preparation time: 55 minutes. Ready to serve: 1 hour, 45 minutes.

Per serving: 710 calories, 40 g total fat (10.5 g saturated fat), 135 mg cholesterol, 2000 mg sodium, 3.5 g fiber.

CIDER-MARINATED VENISON LOIN

A venison loin benefits from a deep marinade (here, a spiced apple cider) and quick cooking. The loin must be trimmed of all silver skin, which can cause it to curl into a ball when cooked.

VENISON

1	(2½-lb.) center-cut venison loin, trimmed
½	teaspoon salt
½	teaspoon freshly ground pepper
8	whole cloves
	Vegetable oil for grill gate

MARINADE

1½	cups apple cider
¼	cup pasteurized orange juice
¼	cup maple syrup
2	tablespoons walnut oil
1	tablespoon Dijon mustard
½	teaspoon ground cinnamon
¼	teaspoon grated nutmeg
¼	teaspoon ground cloves

1 **For Venison:** Tie loin in 3 places along its length with butcher twine, so it stays round when cooked. Place in medium baking dish; sprinkle with salt, pepper and cloves.

2 **For Marinade:** In medium bowl, whisk apple cider, orange juice, maple syrup, walnut oil, Dijon, cinnamon, nutmeg and ground cloves until smooth; pour over venison loin. Turn to coat, then gently massage marinade into meat. Cover; refrigerate at least 8 hours but no more than 24 hours, turning occasionally.

3 Heat grill for direct cooking. Drain meat; reserve marinade. Do not blot dry. Let meat stand at room temperature while grill heats.

4 Brush grill grate with oil. Place venison loin on gas grill directly over high heat or on charcoal grill 4 to 6 inches directly over high coals. Grill, turning occasionally and mopping with reserved marinade during the first 20 minutes of cooking, 22 to 28 minutes or until lightly browned and meat thermometer inserted into thickest part of loin registers 145°F for medium-rare or 160°F for medium. (Do not cook venison loin above medium; it will toughen considerably.) Transfer to carving board; let rest 5 minutes. Slice into ½-inch strips against the grain.

6 servings.

Preparation time: 8 hours, 25 minutes. Ready to serve: 8 hours, 45 minutes.

Per serving: 275 calories, 7 g total fat (2 g saturated fat), 155 mg cholesterol, 190 mg sodium, 0 g fiber.

APRICOT GRILLED PHEASANT WITHA GRILLED APRICOT RELISH

A true delicacy, pheasant is rich, moist (when cooked right), light, yet somehow earthy as well: sophisticated and rustic all at once. You can see the picture for this recipe in full glory on pages 96-97.

APRICOT MARINADE
1 (30-oz.) can apricot halves in heavy syrup, drained
1½ cups dry vermouth
2 teaspoons salt
¼ teaspoon cayenne pepper

PHEASANT
1 (3- to 4-lb.) pheasant, cleaned, rinsed
3 sprigs rosemary
⅓ lb. pancetta, thinly sliced
   Vegetable oil for grill grate

GRILLED APRICOT RELISH
2 tablespoons olive oil, plus additional for grill grate
4 ripe fresh apricots, pitted, halved
½ cup green grapes, halved
1 small red or green bell pepper, chopped
½ small red onion, finely chopped
1 tablespoon Champagne vinegar or white wine vinegar
1 tablespoon chopped fresh parsley
1 teaspoon salt

1   **For Marinade:** In food processor or blender, puree all ingredients until smooth. In large baking dish, combine marinade and pheasant; turn to coat. Cover; refrigerate at least 6 hours but no more than 24 hours, turning occasionally.

2   **For Pheasant:** Arrange grill for indirect cooking with drip pan under unheated portion of grill grate. Heat grill. Meanwhile, drain pheasant; reserve marinade. Place 1 sprig of the rosemary in body cavity. Tie legs together with butcher twine. Lay remaining 2 sprigs rosemary on top of breast. Unwind pancetta slices into strips; lay over rosemary and breast meat. The pancetta will overlap sides of bird. Using butcher twine, secure pancetta to bird — begin at the legs and wrap twine around body, tying closed under legs.

3   Brush grill grate with oil. Place pheasant breast-side down on gas grill over drip pan, indirectly over medium heat; or on charcoal grill over drip pan, but to the side of medium-hot coals. Cover; barbecue 45 Ωreserved marinade.

4   Turn breast-side up. Cover; barbecue undisturbed 50 minutes to 1 hour 10 minutes or until pancetta is brown and meat thermometer inserted in thickest part of thigh registers 160°F (the juices will run pink).

5   Transfer pheasant to carving board. Maintain grill temperature. Let bird rest 5 minutes before removing twine. Remove pancetta and rosemary. (Pancetta may be discarded or served alongside as crackling; rosemary may be discarded or used for platter decoration.)

6   Mop breast with marinade; place pheasant breast-side down on grill directly over medium heat. Grill 3 to 5 minutes or until crisp. Transfer to carving board; let rest 5 minutes before carving.

7   **Meanwhile, prepare Relish:** Heat grill for direct cooking. Brush grill grate with oil. Place apricot halves on gas grill directly over medium heat or on charcoal grill 4 to 6 inches from medium-hot coals. Grill, turning once, 4 to 6 minutes or until lightly browned. Transfer to cutting board; let stand 5 minutes. Roughly chop; place in medium bowl.

8   Stir in olive oil, grapes, bell pepper, red onion, vinegar, parsley and 1 teaspoon salt until well combined. Set aside, covered, at room temperature up to 4 hours, until pheasant is cooked. Relish can be prepared ahead. Store, covered, in refrigerator up to 4 days. Return to room temperature; stir thoroughly before serving.

4 servings.

Preparation time: 1 hour. Ready to serve: 1 hour, 45 minutes.

Per serving: 470 calories, 20 g total fat (6 g saturated fat), 130 mg cholesterol, 920 mg sodium, 1.5 g fiber.

MARTINI-MARINATED VENISON STEAKS

A martini and a venison steak are a fantastic duo. So why not combine the two in one dish? Gin is made with juniper berries — their piney taste blends with the meat while it marinates. If you're in the mood for a "dirty" martini, add 1 tablespoon olive brine, the liquid in jarred, vinegared olives, to the marinade; but if you do, marinate steaks no more than four hours.

2 (1-lb.) venison steaks, preferably sirloin

1 cup plus 1 tablespoon gin*

¼ cup dry vermouth

2 tablespoons olive oil, plus additional for grill grate

1 teaspoon salt

1 teaspoon freshly ground pepper

1 Place steaks in large resealable plastic bag. Add 1 cup of the gin and vermouth. Seal bag; shake well. Refrigerate at least 4 hours but no more than 8 hours.

2 Heat grill for direct cooking. Remove steaks from marinade, blotting dry with paper towels; discard marinade. Rub 1 tablespoon olive oil, ½ teaspoon salt and ½ teaspoon pepper into each steak.

3 Brush grill grate with oil. Place steaks on gas grill directly over high heat or on charcoal grill 4 to 6 inches directly over high-heat coals. Drizzle with remaining 1 tablespoon gin (be careful of flames). Cover; grill, turning once, 15 to 18 minutes or until lightly charred or until meat thermometer inserted into thickest part of steak registers 140°F for rare, 145°F for medium-rare (preferred doneness) or 160°F for medium. Transfer to carving board; let rest 5 minutes. Carve each steak into halves or slice into 1-inch-thick pieces against the grain.

4 servings.

Preparation time: 4 hours, 20 minutes. Ready to serve: 4 hours, 35 minutes.

Per serving: 280 calories, 11 g total fat (2.5 g saturated fat), 150 mg cholesterol, 655 mg sodium, 0 g fiber.

TIP *For a subtle flavor that is not overpoweringly alcoholic, use the highest quality gin you can afford. Boodles and Tanqueray are two we recommend.

BARBECUED WILD DUCK WITH A CHUNKY SOUR CHERRY SAUCE

Wild ducks are fattier than farm-raised, partly because the wild ones have to survive in frigid waters. A mallard would be the best choice for this recipe. The accompanying cherry sauce is sour and savory, a good match for this hearty game bird.

DUCK

1 (6- to 8-lb.) wild duck, cleaned, trimmed of excess visible fat

MARINADE

1 (14.5-oz.) can tart cherries in water, drained, water reserved

⅓ cup soy sauce

2 tablespoons rice vinegar or cider vinegar

3 tablespoons plus 1 teaspoon honey, preferably dark
   Vegetable oil for grill gate

CHUNKY SOUR CHERRY SAUCE

2 green onions, chopped

⅓ cup packed shredded fresh basil

¼ cup each chili sauce, dry vermouth, red wine vinegar, chopped slivered almonds

1 teaspoon minced fresh mint

½ teaspoon salt

1 Tie duck legs together; prick duck all over with meat fork, taking care to pierce only skin and fat, not meat. Place in large baking dish or Dutch oven. **For Marinade:** In small bowl, whisk reserved cherry water, soy sauce, rice vinegar and 2 tablespoons of the honey until smooth. Pour inside and over duck. Cover; refrigerate at least 6 hours but no more than 24 hours, basting occasionally.

2 **To make Sauce:** In medium saucepan, bring drained cherries, remaining 1 tablespoon plus 1 teaspoon honey, green onions, basil, chili sauce, vermouth, red wine vinegar, almonds, mint and salt to a simmer over medium heat. Reduce heat to low; simmer uncovered 15 minutes or until thickened, stirring often to break up cherries. Cherry sauce can be prepared ahead. Store, covered, in refrigerator up to 1 week; bring to room temperature before serving.

3 Arrange grill for indirect cooking with drip pan under unheated portion of grill grate. Heat grill. Let duck and marinade stand at room temperature while grill heats. Brush grill grate with oil. Remove duck from marinade; reserve marinade. Place duck breast- side down on gas grill over drip pan, but indirectly over medium heat; or on charcoal grill over drip pan, but to the side of medium-hot coals. Cover; grill 1 hour undisturbed.

4 Turn breast-side up. Cover; grill, basting every 15 minutes with reserved marinade, about 1 hour or until well browned and meat thermometer inserted halfway into breast meat registers 165°F for medium (preferred doneness) or 175°F for well-done. (In either case, the juices will run pink.) Transfer duck to carving board; let stand 5 minutes. Carve; serve with reserved cherry sauce.

6 servings.

Preparation time: 6 hours, 55 minutes. Ready to serve: 8 hours, 45 minutes.

Per serving: 435 calories, 20 g total fat (5.5 g saturated fat), 120 mg cholesterol, 900 mg sodium, 2 g fiber.

WILD TURKEY WITH MOLE

Because it is so low in fat, a wild turkey must be brined before it's cooked on the grill. This brine is simply salt and water — other spices would conflict with Mole (page 107), a traditional Mexican sauce made with cocoa powder and three kinds of dried chiles, all available in gourmet markets or Latin American grocery stores. If you've never cooked a wild turkey or had mole, you're in for quite a treat. Just be forewarned that wild turkeys do not possess the gargantuan breasts their barnyard cousins do.

1 (7- to 8-lb.) wild turkey, cleaned, thoroughly rinsed*
4 cups warm water
1½ cups salt
1 medium onion, halved
1 medium orange, quartered
1½ lb. thin-sliced bacon
   Vegetable oil for grill grate

1 Set turkey in stockpot large enough to hold it, submerging it in cold water. In medium bowl, whisk warm water and salt until salt dissolves. Pour over turkey. Add enough cold water to pot to cover turkey. Cover; refrigerate at least 12 hours but no more than 24 hours.

2 Arrange grill for indirect cooking with drip pan under unheated portion of grill grate. Heat grill.

3 Meanwhile, drain turkey. Rinse; pat dry with paper towels. Stuff with onion and orange. Tie legs together with butcher twine; tie wings against breast to protect meat. Lay ¾ lb. of the bacon over exposed breast meat, overlapping each slice by half and allowing slices to hang down onto sides of breast. Lay remaining ½ lb. bacon over thighs and legs.

4 Brush grill grate with oil. Place turkey breast-side up on gas grill over drip pan, indirectly over medium heat; or on charcoal grill over drip pan, but to the side of medium-hot coals. Cover; barbecue 3 to 3½ hours or until well browned and meat thermometer inserted halfway into thickest part of breast registers 160°F for medium (preferred doneness) or 180°F for well-done. (In any event, the juices will run pink.) Transfer turkey to carving board; let rest 5 minutes. Discard onion and orange; remove bacon before carving.

6 servings.

Preparation time: 13 hours, 40 minutes. Ready to serve: 16 hours, 10 minutes.

Per serving: 505 calories, 25 g total fat (7 g saturated fat), 135 mg cholesterol, 1175 mg sodium, 3.5 g fiber.

TIP *The only wild turkeys of this approximate size are young-of-the-year birds shot in fall hunting seasons. They are delicious. Turkeys are also hunted in spring, but only adult males are shot then, and they can weigh up to 20 or more pounds!

MOLE

- 4 dried ancho chiles, stemmed, seeded
- 4 dried mulato chiles, stemmed, seeded
- 4 dried pasilla chiles, stemmed, seeded
- 4 cups boiling water
- 4 dried plums (prunes)
- 5 medium plum tomatoes, cut into halves
- 2 tablespoons sesame seeds
- ¼ cup shelled, unsalted, raw pumpkin seeds (also called pepitas)
- 2 tablespoons sliced almonds
- 1 teaspoon peanut oil
- 1 ripe plantain, peeled, cut into ½-inch-thick rounds
- 3 garlic cloves, cut into quarters
- 2 cups reduced-sodium chicken broth, plus additional for thinning sauce
- 2 tablespoons shortening or lard
- 1 tablespoon ground cinnamon
- 1 teaspoon salt
- ½ teaspoon freshly ground pepper
- ¼ teaspoon ground allspice
- 2 oz. unsweetened chocolate, chopped
- 1 tablespoon honey

1 Heat oven to 400°F. Break chile skins into large pieces; place on large baking sheet in single layer. Bake 4 minutes or until fragrant. Transfer to large bowl; cover with 3 cups of the boiling water. Steep 10 minutes.

2 In small bowl, cover dried plums with remaining 1 cup boiling water. Steep 10 minutes. Meanwhile, heat broiler. Place tomatoes on medium-lipped baking sheet; broil until charred, about 5 minutes, turning to blacken all over. Transfer to large bowl.

3 In small skillet, cook sesame seeds over medium heat 3 minutes or until fragrant and lightly browned, stirring constantly. Add sesame seeds to tomatoes. Return skillet to medium heat; add pumpkin seeds. Cook 2 minutes or until seeds pop and are lightly browned, stirring frequently. Add to tomato mixture. Return skillet to medium heat; add almonds. Cook 1 minute or until lightly browned, stirring frequently. Add to tomato mixture. Return skillet to medium heat; swirl in peanut oil. When oil is hot, add plantain rounds in 1 layer. Cook 2 minutes or until lightly browned. Turn; add garlic. Cook 2 minutes or until plantains are tender and lightly browned. Transfer to tomato mixture.

4 Drain chiles and dried plums; add to tomato mixture. Stir until well combined. Puree in food processor or blender until fairly smooth (some nuts and seeds will not fully break down), adding just enough broth to allow mixture to blend. Use only as much broth as necessary for each batch to puree.

5 In high-sided pot or Dutch oven, melt shortening over medium heat. Add puree along with any remaining broth, cinnamon, salt, pepper and allspice. Stir until incorporated and mixture comes to a simmer. Reduce heat to low; add chocolate and honey. Cook 10 minutes or until thick and slightly grainy, stirring constantly. Before serving, thin mole with additional broth until consistency of thick spaghetti sauce.

110 calories, 6 g fat (2 g saturated fat), 0 mg cholesterol, 210 mg sodium, 3 g fiber.

VENISON BURGERS WITH HORSERADISH MAYONNAISE

As any hunter knows, you end up with more ground venison than any of the more spectacular cuts. So venison burgers naturally become a staple during the long winter months after hunting season. Cook venison burgers, as you would all ground meat, until well-done.

BURGERS
1½ lb. ground venison
1   tablespoon each Dijon mustard, Worcestershire sauce, dehydrated minced onion
1   teaspoon salt
¾   teaspoon finely ground pepper
4   drops hot pepper sauce, or to taste
4   hamburger buns, kaiser rolls or English muffins, split
1   teaspoon vegetable oil, plus additional for grill grate

HORSERADISH MAYONNAISE
½   cup mayonnaise (regular, low-fat or nonfat)
1   tablespoon sour cream (regular, low-fat or nonfat)
1½ teaspoons prepared horseradish
1   teaspoon ginger juice*
½   teaspoon salt
¼   teaspoon freshly ground pepper

1   Heat grill for direct cooking.

2   In large bowl, mix venison, Dijon, Worcestershire, onion, salt, pepper and hot pepper sauce, working spices through meat only until combined. Form into 4 (5-inch) patties, about ⅔ cup each.

3   Brush grill grate with oil. Place burgers on gas grill directly over high heat or on charcoal grill 4 to 6 inches directly over high-heat coals. Grill, turning once, about 13 minutes or until lightly charred and meat thermometer inserted into patty registers 160°F. Transfer to carving board; tent with foil to keep warm, if desired.

4   Brush oil on cut side of buns; place on grate directly over heat. Toast about 1 minute or until golden.

5   Meanwhile, prepare Mayonnaise: In small bowl, stir mayonnaise, sour cream, horseradish, ginger juice, salt and pepper until well mixed. Spread Mayonnaise on buns. Mayonnaise can be prepared ahead. Store, covered, in refrigerator up to 3 days.

4 servings.

Preparation time: 25 minutes. Ready to serve: 40 minutes.

Per serving: 555 calories, 30 g total fat (6 g saturated fat), 160 mg cholesterol, 1430 mg sodium, 2 g fiber.

TIP *Ginger juice is available bottled in most supermarkets, along with other condiments. To make it yourself, press about 1 tablespoon chopped peeled fresh ginger through garlic press.

WINE-MARINATED ELK LOIN WITH HUCKLEBERRY CHUTNEY

Elk may be the most misunderstood American meat — and yet the meat that best represents the American West. Some elk can taste pungent. But with a strong marinade — like this wine marinade reminiscent of that used for boeuf bourguignon *— and very high heat, the results are fantastic: a luxurious dinner.*

WINE MARINADE
- 2 cups red wine
- 3 tablespoons red wine vinegar
- 2 tablespoons juniper berries, crushed
- 1 tablespoon each fresh thyme, chopped fresh rosemary
- 2 teaspoons salt
- ½ teaspoon ground allspice
- 4 bay leaves

ELK
- 1 (4-lb.) elk loin, trimmed*
- ¼ cup peanut oil, plus additional for grill grate
- 1 teaspoon freshly ground pepper

HUCKLEBERRY CHUTNEY
- 1 teaspoon vegetable oil
- 1 medium onion, sliced into thin rings
- 2 garlic cloves, minced
- 1 cup port or Madeira
- 3 cups huckleberries or blueberries**
- 1 cinnamon stick
- ⅔ cup sugar
- ½ cup red wine vinegar
- 1 teaspoon salt
- ⅛ teaspoon cayenne pepper

1 **For Marinade:** In medium bowl, mix 3 tablespoons red wine vinegar, juniper berries, thyme, rosemary, 1 teaspoon of the salt and allspice. Lay bay leaves in large glass baking dish; place elk loin on top. Pour marinade over loin. Cover; refrigerate at least 8 hours but no more than 24 hours, turning occasionally.

2 Heat grill for direct cooking. Remove loin from marinade; discard marinade. Blot loin dry with paper towels; rub peanut oil, 1 teaspoon salt and pepper into meat. Let stand at room temperature while grill heats.

3 Brush grill grate with oil. Place elk loin on gas grill directly over high heat or on charcoal grill 4 to 6 inches directly over high coals. Grill, turning once, 30 minutes or until browned and meat thermometer inserted into thickest part of loin registers 140°F for medium-rare (preferred doneness). Transfer to carving board; let stand 5 minutes. Carve into ½-inch slices. Serve with chutney.

4 **For Chutney:** In medium saucepan, heat vegetable oil over medium heat until hot. Add onion and garlic; sauté 3 minutes or until fragrant. Stir in port, huckleberries and cinnamon stick; bring to a boil. Cover; reduce heat to low. Simmer 20 minutes or until huckleberries break down. Uncover; stir in sugar, ½ cup red wine vinegar, 1 teaspoon salt and cayenne. Increase heat to medium; simmer 5 minutes or until thickened, stirring constantly. Serve warm or at room temperature. Chutney can be prepared ahead. Store, covered, in refrigerator up to 3 days.

8 servings.

Preparation time: 8 hours, 50 minutes. Ready to serve: 9 hours, 20 minutes.

Per serving: 360 calories, 12 g total fat (2.5 g saturated fat), 125 mg cholesterol, 610 mg sodium, 1 g fiber.

TIP *An elk loin has a hard layer of fat and silver skin along one side; remove this or the loin will curl into a ball as it cooks. Use a sharp knife to slip under one short side of the layer of fat. Do not saw; rather, gently and firmly draw the blade back and forth, moving it along the surface of the loin, just under the fat. Use your fingers to pull off any silver skin that still adheres to the meat.

TIP **Huckleberries are relatively hard berries and must be cooked before they can be used. There are bumper crops most years in Wisconsin and Montana. These tart and fragrant berries are admittedly hard to find. If you substitute blueberries, reduce sugar to ½ cup and cook only ten minutes with the port.

Whole Red Snapper Wrapped in Grape Leaves, page 119

FISH

Nothing comes off the grill as fast as fish — and almost nothing comes off so well. These recipes are quick and easy, naturally so. In fact, the first step to many of these recipes is to heat the grill because any fish preparation can take place while the grill is heating. When it comes to fish, "well-done" just isn't. It's better to err on the side of underdone. The days of leaving a piece of salmon on the grill for 30 minutes are long gone. Save the slow roasting and complicated rubs for beef, pork and game. With fish, it's dinner in minutes.

GRILLED TROUT

Trout may well be the simplest meal you can prepare on the grill. Simply add a few herbs and you're ready to eat in under 15 minutes. When buying whole trout (or any whole fish), look at the eyes: They should be clear, lucid and lifelike, with perhaps only a spot or two of blood. Avoid whole fish with milky, opaque or overcast eyes. Best of all — fresh-caught trout from a cold stream or lake!

4	(12-oz.) whole brook or rainbow trout, scaled, gutted and cleaned
1	tablespoon plus 1 teaspoon salt, preferably sea salt or kosher (coarse) salt
2	teaspoons freshly ground pepper
4	sprigs rosemary
4	sprigs thyme
8	sprigs parsley
1/4	cup olive oil, plus additional for grill grate

1 Arrange grill for indirect cooking. Heat grill.

2 Season inside each trout's cavity with 1 teaspoon salt and 1/2 teaspoon pepper. Lay 1 sprig rosemary, 1 sprig thyme and 2 sprigs parsley in each body cavity; close over herbs. Rub 1 tablespoon olive oil into skin of each trout.

3 Brush grill grate with oil. Place trout on gas grill indirectly over medium heat or on charcoal grill over but well to the side of medium-hot coals. Cover; grill, turning once, about 12 minutes or until browned outside but opaque inside.

4 servings.

Preparation time: 10 minutes. Ready to serve: 20 minutes.

Per serving: 260 calories, 18 g total fat (3 g saturated fat), 60 mg cholesterol, 645 mg sodium, 0 g fiber.

GRILLING BASKETS

Fish are so delicate, they can easily break into pieces on the grate; they often benefit from being put in grill baskets. For this recipe, choose baskets long enough to hold whole trout. Oil the basket before placing the trout inside, then set the basket on the grill indirectly over medium heat. Turn as indicated in recipe. Use grilling gloves or a hot pad: The handle of a metal grilling basket can get very hot. Also remember to place the basket so that grill's lid doesn't hit the handle and lift the basket off the grill grate, thus raising it too far above the fire to be of any use.

CURRIED SALMON FILLETS

Here, easy salmon fillets are bathed in a simple curry dressing. For a deeper taste, make the dressing the night before so that it has a chance to mellow in the refrigerator overnight. Since salmon skin sticks badly to a grill grate, oil both it and the grill grate before cooking.

½ cup mayonnaise (regular, low-fat or nonfat)

¼ cup Dijon mustard

1 tablespoon chopped fresh parsley

2 teaspoons curry powder

1 teaspoon packed light brown sugar

1 teaspoon lemon juice

2 tablespoons olive oil, plus additional for grill grate

6 (8-oz.) individual salmon fillets, with skin or 1 (3-lb.) salmon fillet, with skin

1 tablespoon salt

2 teaspoons freshly ground pepper

1 Arrange grill for indirect cooking. Heat grill.

2 In small bowl, combine mayonnaise, Dijon, parsley, curry powder, brown sugar and lemon juice until smooth.

3 Coat salmon skin with olive oil; gently rub salt and pepper into meat. (By rubbing lightly, you can also check for bones. Remove any with tweezers.)

4 Generously brush grill grate with oil. Place salmon fillets skin-side down on gas grill indirectly over high heat or on charcoal grill to the side of high-heat coals. Divide mayonnaise dressing among fillets, spooning over meat to coat but taking care not to get dressing on grill grate. Cover; grill about 15 minutes or until salmon begins to flake and dressing is glazed. To test for doneness, insert metal skewer into meat, then touch side of skewer to your lips; it should feel warm.* If desired, carefully transfer fillets to hot part of grill grate; place skin-side down to crisp, about 1 minute.

6 servings.

Preparation time: 15 minutes. Ready to serve: 30 minutes.

Per serving: 475 calories, 30 g total fat (6 g saturated fat), 160 mg cholesterol, 660 mg sodium, 0.5 g fiber.

TIP *Salmon is best slightly underdone, with a pink, gelatinous center. (It will continue to cook as it rests on the plate while you sit down to dinner.) If you prefer your fillets well-done, the skewer inserted into the meat should be hot to the touch.

SESAME MOPPED HALIBUT

For meaty halibut, the traditional dipping sauce for Chinese dumplings adapts here to become a mop. It's great for a quick dinner off the grill, any night of the week. This sauce would also be good on grilled tuna, sea bass, salmon, marlin — or even chicken breasts.

SESAME MOP

- 2 green onions, minced
- 2 garlic cloves, minced
- 2 tablespoons minced peeled fresh ginger
- ¼ cup rice vinegar
- ¼ cup soy sauce
- 2 tablespoons dark sesame oil*
- 1 teaspoon chili oil (optional)

HALIBUT

Vegetable oil for grill grate
- 4 (6- to 8-oz.) skinless halibut fillets, or 4 (8-oz.) halibut steaks

1 Heat grill for direct cooking.

2 **For Mop:** In blender or food processor, pulse green onions, garlic, ginger, rice vinegar, soy sauce, sesame oil and chili oil, if using, until smooth.

3 **For Halibut:** Generously brush grill grate with oil. Place halibut on gas grill directly over high heat or on charcoal grill directly over high-heat coals. Alternately, oil fish basket; place halibut in basket to grill directly over high heat. Mop generously with mop. Cover; grill, mopping frequently and turning once, about 9 minutes for fillets (12 for steaks) or until flesh is firm and opaque. Fillets are fragile; if large, use 2 spatulas to remove from grill.

4 servings.

Preparation time: 10 minutes.

Ready to serve: 20 minutes.

Per serving: 200 calories, 6 g total fat (1 g saturated fat), 90 mg cholesterol, 655 mg sodium, 0 g fiber.

TIP *Sesame oil is pressed from sesame seeds — the world's oldest spice. It's available in two forms: a light golden oil (sometimes packaged as untoasted) and a dark brown oil (sometimes called toasted). The latter has a deeper, toasted-nut taste.

WHOLE RED SNAPPER WRAPPED IN GRAPE LEAVES

Grape leaves, dill and lemon slices here help seal in the natural juices and protect the fish from the heat, all while infusing it with delicate, Mediterranean flavors. An oiled grill basket makes the fish much easier to turn.

1   (8-oz.) jar grape leaves, drained, rinsed

¾   cup finely chopped fresh dill

1   small lemon, sliced into paper-thin rings

1   (2½-lb.) red snapper, scaled, gutted and cleaned*

2   tablespoons olive oil, plus additional for grill grate

½   teaspoon salt

½   teaspoon freshly ground pepper

¼   cup chopped fresh parsley

1 Heat grill for direct cooking.

2 Lay grape leaves on work surface, overlapping to form a large bed (creating layer of overlapping grape leaves that will encircle the fish). Reserve 15 to 17 large grape leaves for top of fish. Sprinkle ¼ cup of the dill over grape leaves; top with 4 of the lemon slices.

3 Score snapper 3 times on each side by making diagonal cuts about 4 inches long and ½ inch deep in skin. Oil each side of fish with 1 tablespoon oil; sprinkle each side with ¼ teaspoon each salt and pepper. Stuff parsley, ¼ cup of the dill and 4 or 5 of the lemon slices inside snapper's body cavity. Place stuffed fish in middle of grape leaf bed.

4 Arrange remaining lemon slices over top of fish; top with remaining ¼ cup dill, then reserved grape leaves. Fold bottom grape leaves up to cover sides of fish, meeting top grape leaves to seal fish. Pat to adhere. Tie fish in 3 places with butcher twine to enclose in leaves.

5 Generously brush grill grate with oil. Gently transfer fish to gas grill directly over medium heat or to charcoal grill 4 to 6 inches directly over medium-heat coals. Cover; grill, turning once with 2 metal spatulas, 20 to 25 minutes or until leaves are crispy and flesh is opaque or until metal skewer inserted into thick part of fish is warm when touched to your lips. Discard grape leaves and lemon slices to serve.

4 servings.

Preparation time: 20 minutes. Ready to serve: 40 minutes.

Per serving: 150 calories, 8 g total fat (1 g saturated fat), 50 mg cholesterol, 370 mg sodium, 0 g fiber.

TIP *You might try this recipe on any number of whole fish, both freshwater and salt, depending on what is available where you live or what you're able to catch. If possible, use a 2- to 3-lb. fish, such as largemouth bass, walleye, redfish, pompano, dorado or parrot fish.

TUNA STEAKS WITH A SWEET-AND-SOUR MOP

COOKING TECHNIQUE: DIRECT, HIGH HEAT

Look no further for a simple but delicious preparation for tuna. Tuna steaks are one of the finest things you can grill: boneless, meaty and tender. Cook fresh tuna to medium-rare with a pink center — or just a little more if you're squeamish about rare fish. Any more time over the heat, and the meat toughens considerably and starts to resemble canned tuna.

TUNA

1½ tablespoons cracked black or green peppercorns

4 (6- to 8-oz.) tuna steaks, about 1 inch thick*

SWEET-AND-SOUR MOP

¼ cup lemon juice

¼ cup soy sauce

¼ cup honey

Vegetable oil for grill grate

1 For Tuna: Heat grill for direct cooking. Gently press cracked peppercorns into tuna.

2 For Mop: In medium bowl, whisk lemon juice, soy sauce and honey until smooth.

3 Brush grill grate with oil. Place tuna steaks on gas grill directly over high heat or on charcoal grill 4 to 6 inches directly over high-heat coals. Mop with mop. Cover; grill, turning once and mopping frequently, 6 minutes for medium-rare (preferred doneness) or 8 minutes for medium.

4 servings.

Preparation time: 10 minutes. Ready to serve: 20 minutes.

Per serving: 285 calories, 8.5 g total fat (2 g saturated fat), 65 mg cholesterol, 585 mg sodium, 0.5 g fiber.

TIP *Always ask your fishmonger if you can smell tuna steaks before you buy them. They should smell fresh and clean, like the ocean, not like the tidal flats. In fact, all fresh ocean fish should smell briny but bright, never oily.

CHECKING FOR DONENESS

Fish cooks quickly. Even one minute can make a big difference. Because it's mostly protein, fish has little natural fat to keep it moist. Try this simple technique with a metal skewer: insert it into the fleshy part of the fish, hold it there 10 seconds, then touch the side of the skewer to your lips. It should feel warm if the fish is medium-rare to medium, or hot if well-done.

FISH IN A PACKET

In a traditional French technique, fish is baked in a parchment-paper envelope. Of course, there's no way to set a paper packet on the grill — unless you cover it in foil to protect it. Have your fishmonger remove the skin from the fillets because it can curl during this quick-cooking method. Remove the foil and serve the paper packets on your guests' plates. They will open the packets and discover this simple and elegant preparation.

4 (8-oz.) white fish fillets, scaled, gutted and cleaned (red snapper, tilapia, bass, whitefish, crappie or a combination)

¼ cup (½ stick) unsalted butter, at room temperature

¼ cup sliced almonds

1 tablespoon plus 1 teaspoon lemon juice

16 cherry tomatoes, halved

4 sprigs parsley

4 sprigs tarragon

4 sprigs thyme

4 garlic cloves, minced

2 teaspoons salt

1 Heat grill for direct cooking.

2 Lay 4 (10-inch) pieces aluminum foil on work surface. Lay similarly sized piece of parchment paper over foil. Lay 1 fish fillet on each. If using combination of fillets, divide among packets so each gets a portion of each fish. Top

each with 1 tablespoon butter, 1 tablespoon almonds, 1 teaspoon lemon juice, 8 tomato halves, 1 sprig parsley, 1 sprig tarragon, 1 sprig thyme, 1 minced garlic clove and ½ teaspoon salt. Fold parchment on all sides to seal and collect juices; seal foil over parchment.

3 Place packets on gas grill directly over high heat or on charcoal grill 4 to 6 inches directly over high-heat coals. Cover; grill 12 minutes or until fish flakes with a fork. Transfer to carving board; let stand 5 minutes before serving.

4 servings.

Preparation time: 20 minutes. Ready to serve: 40 minutes.

Per serving: 335 calories, 17 g total fat (8 g saturated fat), 135 mg cholesterol, 1335 mg sodium, 1.5 g fiber.

SALMON BURGERS

These fresh, light patties have begun to show up at fish counters across the country. But why pay retail when they're so easy to make at home? Pulse the salmon in the food processor just until it looks like ground turkey, so that the cakes will have some tooth when they're cooked. Serve Salmon Burgers *on their own, in hamburger buns with traditional burger condiments or in pita pockets with ranch dressing, shredded lettuce and diced tomato.*

1	lb. boneless skinless salmon fillet, cut into 3 pieces*
1	egg white, lightly beaten
1/3	cup plain dry bread crumbs
1	green onion, minced
2	tablespoons mayonnaise (regular or low-fat)
1	tablespoon chopped fresh dill
2	teaspoons celery seed
1	teaspoon lemon juice
1	teaspoon sweet paprika
1	teaspoon freshly ground pepper
1/2	teaspoon salt
	Vegetable oil for grill grate

1 Heat grill for direct cooking.

2 In food processor, pulse salmon until coarsely chopped. Add egg white; pulse twice, just to incorporate. Alternatively, you can chop salmon by hand: Place on clean work surface and use 2 sharp chef's knives (1 in each hand) to chop, remounding it as necessary before chopping in egg white.

3 Transfer salmon mixture to large bowl; stir in bread crumbs, green onion, mayonnaise, dill, celery seed, lemon juice, paprika, pepper and salt. Form into 4 (5-inch) patties; gently pat until firm.

4 Brush grill grate with oil. Place patties on gas grill directly over high heat or on charcoal grill 4 to 6 inches directly over high-heat coals. Grill, turning once with metal spatula, 6 to 7 minutes or until golden.

4 servings.

Preparation time: 20 minutes. Ready to serve: 30 minutes.

Per serving: 260 calories, 12.5 g total fat (2.5 g saturated fat), 75 mg cholesterol, 490 mg sodium, 0.5 g fiber.

TIP *Have your fishmonger remove the skin from the salmon for you. It must be cut off so that the meat processes smoothly in the food processor. Before you chop the salmon, run your fingers slowly across fillet to check for bones. Remove any with tweezers. Do not use canned salmon — you need the gelatinous quality of fresh fish to hold these patties together.

FISH TACOS

Okay, it sounds odd — but Fish Tacos *are taking many areas of the country by storm. Here, cod fillets are marinated in ranch dressing, then grilled, before becoming part of a barbecue-sauced taco. It's an easy meal — and one that won't sound odd once you try it.*

FISH
1 lb. cod fillet
1 (8-oz.) bottle ranch dressing
   Vegetable oil for grill grate

TACOS
12 taco shells
½ cup bottled barbecue sauce

GARNISH
   Shredded cheddar cheese
   Shredded lettuce
   Diced tomatoes

1 Place fillet in large baking dish; coat with dressing. Cover; refrigerate at least 2 hours but no more than 6 hours, turning occasionally.

2 Heat grill for direct cooking.

3 Remove cod from marinade; do not blot dry, allowing any excess to fall into baking dish. Discard excess.

4 Brush grill grate with oil. Place cod on gas grill directly over high heat or on charcoal grill directly over high-heat coals. Alternatively, place cod fillets in grilling basket. Cover; grill, turning once with spatula, 5 minutes or until fish flakes easily with a fork and coating browns lightly

5 Transfer to carving board; slice into 12 servings. Place in taco shells; top with 2 teaspoons barbecue sauce, cheese, lettuce and tomatoes.

6 servings.

Preparation time: 10 minutes. Ready to serve: 2 hours, 15 minutes.

Per serving: 315 calories, 16.5 g total fat (4.5 g saturated fat), 55 mg cholesterol, 500 mg sodium, 3 g fiber.

GRILLED OYSTERS ROCKEFELLER

On Point Reyes, that stretch of sea-beaten land extending into the Pacific north of San Francisco, locals take bags of fresh oysters to the beaches, build huge pits and barbecue the oysters. But why stop there? A bread crumb topping turns these grilled oysters into a Rockefeller concoction.

3 tablespoons unsalted butter, melted, cooled

½ cup plain dry bread crumbs

2 green onions, minced

1 garlic clove, minced

2 tablespoons minced fresh parsley

2 tablespoons Pernod, Pastis or other licorice liqueur

1 teaspoon freshly ground pepper

¼ teaspoon salt

3 drops hot pepper sauce or more to taste

¼ cup (1 oz.) freshly grated Parmesan cheese

2 dozen large fresh oysters*

1 In medium bowl, mix butter, bread crumbs, green onions, garlic, parsley, liqueur, pepper, salt and hot pepper sauce until uniform and moist.

2 Heat grill for direct cooking. Do not prepare oysters until grill is hot.

3 Wear large oven mitt or wrap arm in dish towel to protect hand while shucking oysters. Shuck oysters by holding in one hand and inserting oyster shucker or small, heavy-duty, flat-head, clean screwdriver into joints of the 2 shells, the tiny pivot points at the small, tapering ends of the shells (where oysters would be hanging off a tree if they were pears). Be careful not to chip shells. Pry open by twisting shucker in pivot points and wrenching shells apart. Clean out any fractured shell bits, then run shucker under oyster meat to cut off inside of shells. Place meat and any accumulated juices in larger halves of shells; discard smaller halves. Divide bread crumb topping among oysters; sprinkle each with Parmesan.

4 Place oysters shell-side down on gas grill directly over high heat or on charcoal grill 4 to 6 inches directly over high-heat coals. Cover; grill undisturbed 5 minutes or until Parmesan melts and topping browns.

4 servings.

Preparation time: 40 minutes. Ready to serve: 50 minutes.

Per serving: 175 calories, 9.5 g total fat (5 g saturated fat), 60 mg cholesterol, 430 mg sodium, 0.5 g fiber.

TIP *Oysters should always smell like an ocean breeze, never fishy, like cod liver oil. You can also tell how fresh they are by tapping the shells: If they are open slightly, they should close immediately; if the shell does not close, discard the oyster. Store oysters in the refrigerator in large bowl lined with and covered loosely by damp paper towels.

WHOLE GRILLED LOBSTER WITH CLARIFIED VANILLA BUTTER

When lobster is grilled, it turns slightly sweet and very aromatic. If you par-boil lobsters first, there's no need to cut them in half live before they go on the grill, a gruesome task for most of us. The Clarified Vanilla Butter is a new American twist on drawn butter, that old favorite lobster "sauce."

LOBSTERS

2   (1½-lb.) lobsters
    Vegetable oil for grill grate

CLARIFIED VANILLA BUTTER

½   cup (1 stick) unsalted butter, softened
½   vanilla bean
1   teaspoon salt
¼   teaspoon sugar

1 **For Lobsters:** Stopper sink; fill halfway with ice water. Bring large pot of salted water to boil over high heat. Plunge lobsters, head first, into boiling water. Cook 2 minutes, until they stop moving. Remove with tongs; plunge into ice water. Cool in ice water 5 minutes.

2 Heat grill for direct cooking. Drain lobsters on paper towels. Divide clarified vanilla butter in half, reserving half at room temperature for dipping sauce.

3 To cut lobsters in half, place on cutting board or work surface "belly-side" down. With cleaver or heavy knife, pierce shells just behind the heads, then slice back and through heads. Remove knife, turn lobsters around and cut back from same point to end of the tails.

4 Brush grill grate with oil. Place lobster halves meat-side down on gas grill directly over high heat or on charcoal grill 4 to 6 inches directly over high coals. Cover; grill 2 minutes. Turn shell-side down; grill, brushing meat frequently with clarified vanilla butter, 6 minutes or until lobsters are heated through. Serve with reserved vanilla butter on the side.

5 **For Butter:** In small saucepan, melt butter over low heat. Remove from heat; let stand 5 minutes. Skim foam off top of butter using small spoon. Slowly pour clear butter from pan into small bowl, leaving milk solids in bottom of saucepan. Discard milk solids.

6 Split vanilla bean in half lengthwise; scrape seeds with knife into clarified butter. Stir in salt and sugar until sugar dissolves. Set aside at room temperature 2 hours to infuse. Butter can be prepared ahead. Store, tightly covered, in refrigerator up to 1 week. Melt solidified butter over low heat in small saucepan, or microwave at Medium for 2 minutes.

2 servings.

Preparation time: 20 minutes. Ready to serve: 2 hours.

Per serving: 540 calories, 42 g total fat (25.5 g saturated fat), 240 mg cholesterol, 1840 mg sodium, 0 g fiber.

SWORDFISH KABOBS WITH A WALNUT PAPRIKA BARBECUE SAUCE

Swordfish is one of the few fish that can be skewered — undoubtedly why it has become a backyard favorite. This unusual barbecue sauce is made with walnuts, paprika and beer — an exotic but aromatic combination.

WALNUT PAPRIKA BARBECUE SAUCE

- ¾ cup beer, preferably wheat or amber beer
- ¼ cup chopped walnuts
- 2 tablespoons walnut oil*
- 2 tablespoons sweet paprika
- 1½ teaspoons sugar
- ½ teaspoon salt
- ¼ teaspoon finely ground pepper

KABOBS

- 1½ lb. swordfish steaks, cut into 16 (2-inch) cubes
- 12 button or cremini mushrooms, cleaned
- 4 zucchini, cut into 2-inch pieces
- Vegetable oil for grill grate

1 **For Sauce:** In blender or food processor, pulse beer, walnuts, walnut oil, paprika, sugar, salt and pepper until smooth.

2 In medium baking dish, cover swordfish cubes with sauce; toss to coat. Cover; refrigerate at least 30 minutes but no more than 3 hours, tossing occasionally.

3 Heat grill for direct cooking.

4 **For Kabobs:** Remove fish from sauce; reserve sauce. Thread 4 pieces fish, 3 mushrooms and 4 pieces zucchini on each water-soaked metal skewer, alternating vegetables and fish. If using bamboo skewers, thread 2 pieces fish, 2 pieces zucchini and 1 or 2 mushrooms on each water-soaked skewer; wrap exposed ends of bamboo skewers in aluminum foil.

5 Brush grill grate with oil. Place skewers on gas grill directly over high heat or on charcoal grill directly over high-heat coals. Cover; grill, turning once and mopping frequently with reserved sauce during first few minutes of cooking, 8 minutes or until swordfish flakes with fork. Transfer to carving board; let rest 5 minutes.

4 servings.

Preparation time: 25 minutes. Ready to serve: 1 hour, 10 minutes.

Per serving: 290 calories, 14 g total fat (3 g saturated fat), 90 mg cholesterol, 235 mg sodium, 2.5 g fiber.

TIP *Always smell walnut oil before using to make sure it hasn't gone rancid. It should smell delicate, not powerful and biting with that musky odor walnuts get when they go bad. Store walnut oil in the refrigerator for a longer shelf life — up to about 4 months — but bring to room temperature before using.

GRILLED SCALLOPS WITH YELLOW PEPPER RELISH

COOKING TECHNIQUE: DIRECT, MEDIUM HEAT

Scallops on the grill are done in minutes; their natural sweetness caramelizes over high heat. The only problem? They tend to dry out because they have almost no natural fat. It's best to marinate them in oil first.

SCALLOPS

24 large sea scallops (about 1½ lb.), cleaned*
2 tablespoons olive oil
1 teaspoon salt
½ teaspoon freshly ground pepper

YELLOW PEPPER RELISH

2 yellow bell peppers, cut into quarters
1 small onion
4 cups boiling water
½ cup lukewarm water
½ cup plus 2 tablespoons white vinegar
3 tablespoons sugar
¼ teaspoon salt
¼ teaspoon crushed red pepper

1 Heat grill for direct cooking.

2 **For Scallops:** Place scallops in large resealable plastic bag; pour in olive oil, 1 teaspoon salt and ground pepper. Seal bag; toss gently to coat. Set aside at room temperature to marinate 10 minutes.

3 Place scallops on gas grill directly over medium heat or on charcoal grill 4 to 6 inches directly over medium-hot coals. Grill, turning once, 4 to 5 minutes or until scallops are opaque and barely firm to the touch.

4 **For Relish:** Shred bell peppers and onion using large holes of box grater or food processor fitted with shredding blade. Place in large bowl; cover with boiling water. Let stand 5 minutes; drain.

5 In medium saucepan, bring bell pepper mixture, lukewarm water and ½ cup of the vinegar to a simmer over high heat. Remove from heat, cover. Let stand 10 minutes; drain.

6 Return pepper mixture to saucepan. Stir in remaining 2 tablespoons vinegar, sugar, ¼ teaspoon salt and crushed red pepper. Bring to a simmer over medium-high heat. Reduce heat to low; simmer 10 minutes or until thickened like marmalade, stirring often. Relish can be prepared ahead. Store, covered, in refrigerator up to 1 week.

4 servings.

Preparation time: 10 minutes. Ready to serve: 25 minutes.

Per serving: 220 calories, 8 g total fat (1 g saturated fat), 30 mg cholesterol, 965 mg sodium, 1 g fiber.

TIP *Scallops have a small muscle that arcs over one side of the meat. This muscle is sometimes cleaned by the fishmonger; but if you live near the coast, or find particularly fresh scallops, it may still be attached. Slice it off — or have your fishmonger thoroughly clean the scallops for you.

MARGARITA GRILLED SHRIMP

Here's a great alternative to hot dogs and burgers. You can also use 1½ cups margarita mix if you'd rather forgo any alcohol.

1   cup tequila, preferably 100% blue agave

¼   cup Cointreau, Triple Sec or other orange-flavored liqueur

¼   cup plus 1 tablespoon lime juice

32   shelled, deveined uncooked large shrimp*

2   tablespoons salt, preferably sea salt or kosher (coarse) salt

1   teaspoon freshly ground pepper
    Vegetable oil for grill grate

4   limes, cut into quarters

1 In large bowl, whisk tequila, liqueur and lime juice until blended. Add shrimp to marinade; toss to coat. Cover; refrigerate 30 minutes, tossing occasionally. Meanwhile, in small bowl, combine salt and pepper. Heat grill for direct cooking.

2 Brush grill grate with oil. Drain shrimp; discard marinade. Place on gas grill directly over medium heat or on charcoal grill 4 to 6 inches directly over medium-heat coals. Grill 5 minutes or until opaque and firm, turning once.

3 To serve, place shrimp on large platter. Serve alongside salt mixture for dipping and lime wedges for biting, much like tequila shots (dip shrimp, bite lime, eat shrimp).

4 servings.

Preparation time: 15 minutes. Ready to serve: 50 minutes.

Per serving: 105 calories, 1 g total fat (0.5 g saturated fat), 165 mg cholesterol, 1060 mg sodium, 0.5 g fiber.

TIP *Shrimp are sold by the number it takes to make a pound. All other words, like "large" and "jumbo" are simply window-dressing.

STRAIGHTENING YOUR SHRIMP

Shrimp curl naturally as they cook. While it won't affect their taste, some people find it an aesthetic problem. If you do, and want to straighten your shrimp, simply pierce one at the thick end with a bamboo skewer that has been soaked in water for 20 minutes, then drained. Push skewer through the body, without breaking the surface, and out the small tail end, thereby keeping the shrimp straight on the skewer as it grills. You may skewer several shrimp on each bamboo skewer.

VIETNAMESE SHRIMP SKEWERS

This is a traditional Vietnamese snack, served in open-air markets across Southeast Asia. Serve this as an elegant first course or a new and innovative take on lunch — along with a selection of premade dipping sauces, if desired, including Coconut Peanut Dipping Sauce *(page 65), bottled sweet-and-sour sauce or ranch dressing.*

4   (8-inch) pieces sugar cane*
¼   cup plus 2 tablespoons rice flour**
1   lb. shelled, deveined uncooked medium shrimp
2   tablespoons minced pork fat or lard
2   tablespoons chopped fresh cilantro
1   tablespoon minced peeled fresh ginger
1   garlic clove, minced
1   tablespoon fish sauce
    Vegetable oil for grill grate

1 Heat grill for direct cooking. Split each piece of sugar cane into fourths lengthwise to make 16 (8-inch) spears. Place ¼ cup of the rice flour on large, flat plate.

2 In food processor, process shrimp, pork fat, remaining 2 tablespoons rice flour, cilantro, ginger, garlic and fish sauce about 1 minute or until smooth, scraping down sides of bowl as necessary. You may also work by hand: Mound ingredients on cutting board and use 2 large chef's knives (1 in each hand) to chop mixture into gelatinous, smooth paste, remounding as necessary.

3 Wet hands; scoop up a golf-ball size piece of shrimp paste. Wrap around middle of 1 spear sugar cane, squeezing and spreading paste to ¼ inch and covering about 4 inches of spear. Roll molded paste in rice flour; shake off excess. Repeat with remaining paste and spears.

4 Generously brush grill grate with oil. Place shrimp paste-covered spears on gas grill directly over medium heat or on charcoal grill 4 to 6 inches directly over medium-hot coals. Grill, turning on to all sides with tongs or metal spatula, 5 minutes or until lightly browned.

4 servings.

Preparation time: 35 minutes. Ready to serve: 40 minutes.

Per serving: 175 calories, 5 g total fat (2 g saturated fat), 110 mg cholesterol, 295 mg sodium, 0.5 g fiber.

TIP *You must peel fresh sugar cane before using — it is coated with wax as a preservative. If you can't find fresh sugar cane, use 2 (15-oz.) cans, drain them thoroughly and cut sections in half (not into quarters), since they're soft.

TIP **Rice flour is a white flour made from white rice. It's available in most Asian markets and in the Asian section of gourmet markets. Do not confuse it with glutinous rice flour, made from glutinous rice and used mostly for Asian confections.

Grilled Antipasti with No-Fuss Aioli, page 146

VEGETABLES

Summer's bounty finds its home on the grill. Farmers' markets offer the freshest of the season's picks. Neighborhood supermarkets stock their bins with tomatoes, corn, zucchini and eggplant. Maybe you have your own garden and home-grown produce. Vegetables make easy dinners and sides on the grill — they cook fast, and even kids who don't like their veggies will love them off the grill. Double or triple these recipes — as long as your grill's big enough to handle the load.

PORTOBELLO BURGERS WITH HERBES DE PROVENCE RUB

Enormous portobello mushrooms have magic powers — they're so big and meaty, people say they've turned many a carnivore into a vegetarian. When rubbed with an herbes de Provence mixture and served with an olive mustard spread, these juicy burgers are so good that your guests might overlook the steaks you've got going on the other side of the grill!

HERBES DE PROVENCE RUB

2   teaspoons dried basil
2   teaspoons dried parsley
2   teaspoons dried rosemary
2   teaspoons dried thyme
½   teaspoon fennel seeds
¼   teaspoon freshly ground pepper
1   bay leaf
¼   teaspoon lavender (optional)

OLIVE MUSTARD

2   tablespoons Dijon mustard
1   tablespoon mayonnaise
1   teaspoon capers, drained, chopped
6   oil-cured ripe olives, drained, pitted and chopped

BURGERS

4   large portobello mushrooms, stems removed, gills cleaned
1   tablespoon plus 1 teaspoon olive oil, plus additional for grill grate
2   teaspoons salt
4   hamburger buns, kaiser rolls or large potato rolls
    Shredded lettuce

1   **For Rub:** In spice grinder or coffee grinder, grind basil, parsley, rosemary, thyme, fennel seeds, pepper, bay leaf and lavender, if using, until fine powder.

2   Heat grill for direct cooking. Oil each mushroom cap with 1 teaspoon olive oil. Rub each cap with 1½ teaspoons spice rub; sprinkle each with ½ teaspoon salt. Set aside at room temperature to marinate 10 minutes.

3   **For Burgers:** Brush grill grate with oil. Place mushrooms gill-side down on gas grill directly over medium heat or on charcoal grill 4 to 6 inches directly over medium-hot coals. Cover; grill, turning once, 10 minutes or until tender. Transfer to serving platter.

4   **For Mustard:** In small bowl, stir together Dijon, mayonnaise, capers and olives.

5   Brush grill grate with oil again. Place buns cut-side down; toast 1 minute. Serve caps as burger patties in buns with mustard. Garnish with shredded lettuce.

4 servings.

Preparation time: 10 minutes. Ready to serve: 30 minutes.

Per serving: 230 calories, 11 g total fat (2 g saturated fat), 5 mg cholesterol, 1600 mg sodium, 3 g fiber.

GRILLED EGGPLANT PARMESAN SANDWICHES

Eggplant Parmesan is an Italian staple — and now you can feature it at your own backyard barbecue if you make it into this simple sandwich using your favorite bottled marinara sauce and grated Parmesan cheese.

1   medium eggplant, cut into ½-inch-thick slices

2   teaspoons salt

1   (24- to 30-inch) loaf Italian bread or large Ciabatta loaf, halved lengthwise

2   tablespoons olive oil, plus additional for grill grate

2   garlic cloves, halved

⅓   cup bottled marinara sauce

½   cup freshly grated Parmesan cheese

1   Heat grill for direct cooking.

2   Sprinkle both sides of eggplant slices with salt; stand vertically in large colander to drain in sink. Drain 30 minutes; blot slices dry with paper towels.

3   Meanwhile, sprinkle 1 tablespoon olive oil on each cut side of bread. Place bread cut-side down on gas grill directly over high heat or on charcoal grill 4 to 6 inches directly over high-heat coals. Toast 1 minute or until golden. Transfer to carving board; rub cut side of each half with garlic. Set aside, discarding garlic. Maintain grill's heat.

4   Brush grill grate with oil. Place eggplant slices on gas grill directly over high heat or on charcoal grill 4 to 6 inches directly over high-heat coals. Cover; grill 2 minutes. Turn with metal spatula. Spoon 2 teaspoons marinara sauce on each slice; top each with 1 tablespoon Parmesan. Cover; grill about 3 minutes or until Parmesan melts and eggplant is browned. Using spatula, carefully transfer topped eggplant slices to cut side of bread loaf, overlapping as necessary. Top with second half of loaf; cut into 6 sandwiches.

6 servings.

Preparation time: 10 minutes. Ready to serve: 45 minutes.

Per serving: 420 calories, 11.5 g total fat (3.5 g saturated fat), 5 mg cholesterol, 975 mg sodium, 6 g fiber.

GRILLED CORN SALAD

Some people grill corn by placing it in its husks directly on the grilling rack. Unfortunately, the husks absorb the taste of the grill. This preparation lets the corn itself soak up those flavors, a boon to the salad. For a spicy salad, use a fresh poblano chile; for a mild salad, use a bell pepper.

Vegetable oil for grill grate
1   poblano chile or green bell pepper
4   ears corn, husked, silks removed
1   small red onion, halved
1   (6½-oz.) jar pimientos, drained, chopped
2   teaspoons Champagne vinegar or white wine vinegar
1   teaspoon Dijon mustard
2   teaspoons chopped fresh dill
1   teaspoon salt
½   teaspoon freshly ground pepper
3   tablespoons olive oil

1   Heat grill for direct cooking.

2   Brush grill grate with oil. Place poblano, corn and red onion on gas grill directly over high heat or on charcoal grill 4 to 6 inches directly over high-heat coals. Cover; grill, turning occasionally, 12 minutes or until poblano is charred on all sides and corn and onion are browned. If corn browns too quickly, move off direct heat.

3   Place poblano in paper bag and seal, or in small bowl and cover with plastic wrap. Set aside 10 minutes. Cut corn kernels from husks; place in large bowl. Chop onion; place in bowl. Add pimientos; stir to combine.

4   Peel skin off pepper; core, seed and chop. Toss in bowl with corn mixture.

5   In small bowl, whisk vinegar, Dijon, dill, salt and pepper until smooth; whisk in olive oil in thin, steady stream until emulsified. Add to corn salad; toss to coat.

6 servings.

Preparation time: 40 minutes. Ready to serve: 40 minutes.

Per serving: 130 calories, 7.5 g total fat (1 g saturated fat), 0 mg cholesterol, 410 mg sodium, 2 g fiber.

STUFFED BELL PEPPERS

Who doesn't love Stuffed Bell Peppers, *a quick-and-easy dinner? So here they are for the grill — but updated a bit. They're stuffed with a wild rice salad made with pecans, cranberries and chutney. Wild rice isn't rice at all — it's a wild grass grain, native to the Upper Midwest. Buy any blend you prefer and cook it according to package directions.*

6	medium green, red or yellow bell peppers
3	cups cooked wild rice, cooled
½	cup chopped pecans
½	cup mango chutney
½	cup chopped fresh cilantro
¼	cup dried cranberries or currants
2	green onions, minced
½	teaspoon salt
¾	cup (3 oz.) shredded Asiago, Pepper, Pepperjack or Swiss cheese

1 Heat grill for direct cooking.

2 Place peppers on gas grill directly over high heat or on charcoal grill directly over high-heat coals. Cover; grill, gently turning with metal spatula, about 6 minutes or until charred all over. (Do not use tongs — peppers cannot be pierced if they are to be stuffed.) Place peppers in large bowl; seal with plastic wrap. Set aside to steam 10 minutes.

3 Meanwhile, in medium bowl, mix wild rice, pecans, chutney, cilantro, dried cranberries, green onions and salt.

4 Peel peppers; slit each along 1 side, then gently seed. Using slit, stuff each pepper with wild rice mixture. Top each with 2 tablespoons cheese.

5 Place large sheet of aluminum foil on gas grill directly over high heat or on charcoal grill directly over high-heat coals. Place stuffed peppers on foil. Cover; grill 5 minutes or until cheese melts and stuffing is heated through.

6 servings.

Preparation time: 25 minutes. Ready to serve: 35 minutes.

Per serving: 265 calories, 11.5 g total fat (3.5 g saturated fat), 15 mg cholesterol, 575 mg sodium, 4 g fiber.

GRILLED ROMAN SALAD

Grilled lettuce has long been an Italian tradition. Don't core these lettuces before you grill them; that way, they will stay in one piece as they cook. Buy the best aged balsamic vinegar you can afford — some are aged up to 50 years and are thick like maple syrup. You might want to try this with Rib Roast with Grilled Pineapple Poblano Salsa *(page 32).*

½ cup olive oil

1 (1½-lb.) head Romaine lettuce, halved, outer leaves removed

2 (6-oz.) heads radicchio, cut into quarters, outer leaves removed

2 (6-oz.) heads Belgian endive, cut into halves, outer leaves removed

1 teaspoon salt

½ teaspoon freshly ground pepper

2 tablespoons aged balsamic vinegar

1 Heat grill for direct cooking.

2 Pour oil in large baking dish; dip lettuces on all sides into oil just before they go on grill. Place oiled lettuces on gas grill directly over high heat or on charcoal grill 4 to 6 inches directly over high coals. Cover; grill, turning once, 4 to 5 minutes or until lightly browned and slightly wilted.

3 Place lettuces on cutting board. Core, discarding tough center stalk. Shred into 1-inch slices. Place in large serving bowl; toss with salt and pepper. Drizzle balsamic vinegar over salad; toss.

6 servings.

Preparation time: 15 minutes. Ready to serve: 15 minutes.

Per serving: 190 calories, 18.5 g total fat (2.5 g saturated fat), 0 mg cholesterol, 415 mg sodium, 4 g fiber.

GRILLED TOMATOES AND GARLIC

Tomatoes soften quickly on the grill, making a terrific side dish or topping for grilled meats and fish. Here, garlic mellows over the fire, making it the perfect accent to these simple tomatoes.

8 medium tomatoes, cut into halves

4 large garlic cloves

¼ cup olive oil, plus more for grill grate

2 teaspoons salt, preferably sea salt or kosher (coarse) salt

16 basil leaves

1 Heat grill for direct cooking.

2 Place tomatoes and garlic in large bowl. Drizzle with olive oil; sprinkle with salt. Toss gently to coat. Thread garlic cloves on water-soaked bamboo skewers; wrap exposed ends of skewer in aluminum foil.

3 Brush grill grate with oil. Place tomatoes cut-side down and garlic skewer on gas grill directly over high heat or on charcoal grill 4 to 6 inches over high-heat coals.* Cover; grill 3 minutes. Turn tomatoes and garlic with metal spatula; top each tomato half with basil leaf. Grill about 3 minutes or until tomato skins are charred and garlic is browned. Be careful — tomato skins can loosen. Gently transfer tomatoes and garlic to platter.

4 servings.

Preparation time: 20 minutes. Ready to serve: 20 minutes.

Per serving: 175 calories, 14.5 g total fat (2 g saturated fat), 0 mg cholesterol, 1185 mg sodium, 3 g fiber.

TIP *Use a grill basket for the tomatoes, but make sure it is thick enough not to crush them when lid is closed. Oil the basket before adding tomatoes and add the basil to each from the very start.

ROASTED TOMATO SOUP

If you want to make a soup with these ingredients, place tomatoes, basil leaves and garlic cloves (removed from skewer) in food processor. Add 2 cups vegetable stock; pulse just until chunky. Serve warm or at room temperature. If desired, place dollop of crème fraîche, plain yogurt or sour cream in center of bowl.

EMBER BAKED TWICE-GRILLED POTATOES

Roast the spuds directly on top of the lava rocks or on the coals. The potatoes get crispy and charred outside, flaky and moist inside. Then stuff them with a creamy bacon filling, top with cheese, and grill a second time.

4   (8- to 10-oz.) baking potatoes
½   cup heavy cream
2   tablespoons unsalted butter, at room temperature
1   teaspoon sweet paprika
1   teaspoon onion powder
½   teaspoon salt
½   teaspoon freshly ground pepper
4   thick slices bacon, cooked, crumbled
½   cup (2 oz.) shredded cheddar cheese

1 Heat grill for direct cooking.

2 Wrap each potato in 2 feet of aluminum foil, rolling it up in several layers of foil and tightly sealing ends. Place directly on lava rocks or coals. Bake 45 to 60 minutes or until potatoes are soft. Transfer to carving board; let rest 5 minutes before unwrapping. Cool until easily handled.

3 Split potatoes open lengthwise. Scoop insides into large bowl, leaving ⅛-inch flesh against skin. Reserve skins.

4 Beat cream and butter into potato flesh with electric mixer at medium speed; beat in paprika, onion powder, salt and pepper 2 minutes or until creamy. Gently fold in bacon using rubber spatula.

5 Fill reserved potato skins with mashed potato mixture. Sprinkle each stuffed potato half with 1 tablespoon cheddar. Place large sheet aluminum foil on gas grill directly over high heat or on charcoal grill directly over high-heat coals. Place filled potato skins on foil; cover grill. Grill 10 minutes or until cheese is melted and stuffing is heated through.

4 servings.
Preparation time: 10 minutes.
Ready to serve: 1 hour, 30 minutes.

Per serving: 470 calories, 26 g total fat (14.5 g saturated fat), 75 mg cholesterol, 605 mg sodium, 4.5 g fiber.

SWEET POTATOES IN THE FLAMES

Use this cooking technique to roast sweet potatoes directly on lava rocks or coals. Simply wrap 4 (10- to 12-oz.) sweet potatoes each in several layers of foil. Place them on the flame or in the coals and let bake about 1 hour.

GRILLED MASHED POTATOES

Sounds odd? No way. True, you don't mash the potatoes on the grill, but the spuds are browned on the grate before they're mashed. One warning: These mashed potatoes aren't smooth and silky. The crunchy bits of potato and skin blend into the final dish for a great texture contrast. It's a grilled take on a classic side dish.

2 lb. baking potatoes, cut into ½-inch-thick slices

Cold unsalted butter, for rubbing on potatoes

⅓ cup milk (regular, low-fat or nonfat) or heavy cream

¼ cup (½ stick) unsalted butter, at room temperature

¼ cup sour cream (regular, low-fat or nonfat)

2 tablespoons freshly grated Parmesan cheese

1 teaspoon salt

½ teaspoon freshly ground pepper

¼ teaspoon grated nutmeg

Unsalted butter, at room temperature (optional)

1 Heat grill for direct cooking.

2 Rub potato slices with butter. Place slices on gas grill directly over medium heat or on charcoal grill 4 to 6 inches directly over medium-hot coals. Cover; grill, turning once, 30 minutes or until browned and softened. If potatoes brown too quickly, move to cooler portion of grate and cook indirectly until softened.

3 Transfer potatoes to large bowl; add milk and ¼ cup butter. Mash with electric mixer at medium speed 1 minute. Add sour cream, Parmesan, salt, pepper and nutmeg; beat 2 minutes or until fluffy and light. Serve hot with butter, if desired.

6 servings.

Preparation time: 15 minutes. Ready to serve: 45 minutes.

Per serving: 255 calories, 13 g total fat (8 g saturated fat), 35 mg cholesterol, 450 mg sodium, 3 g fiber.

BAKED BEANS

COOKING TECHNIQUE: DIRECT, HIGH HEAT, THEN DIRECT, MEDIUM HEAT

Like the Baked Beans *made at a chuckwagon dinner, these are best right off the grill. Use a heavy pot, preferably cast iron, to cook on the grate. Cover the grill while the beans cook, but don't put a lid on the pot they're in. Slices of ham are usually available in the meat section of your supermarket; if not, have the deli counter slice you a ½-inch-thick slab.*

2 tablespoons vegetable oil
1 medium onion, chopped
1 green bell pepper, chopped
2 garlic cloves, minced
1 (8-oz.) slice precooked boneless ham steak
2 (15-oz.) cans pink or pinto beans, drained, rinsed
1 (15-oz.) can tomato sauce
1 (14-oz.) can reduced-sodium vegetable or chicken broth
½ cup ketchup
2 tablespoons packed light brown sugar
2 tablespoons Dijon mustard
1 tablespoon molasses
1 teaspoon salt
1 teaspoon sweet paprika
½ teaspoon freshly ground pepper
4 drops hot pepper sauce or to taste

1 Heat grill for direct cooking.

2 Heat oil in heavy large pot on gas grill over high heat or on charcoal grill 4 to 6 inches directly over high-heat coals. Add onion, bell pepper and garlic. Cover grill; sauté about 6 minutes or until softened and fragrant, stirring occasionally.

3 Meanwhile, place ham steak on grill over high heat. Cook 5 minutes, turning once. Transfer to carving board; chop. Add to pot with onion mixture.

4 If using gas grill, reduce heat to medium. If using charcoal grill, close vents to reduce heat to medium. Stir in beans, tomato sauce, broth, ketchup, brown sugar, Dijon, molasses, salt, paprika, pepper and hot pepper sauce. Cover grill; cook 1 hour or until thickened, stirring occasionally.

8 servings.

Preparation time: 30 minutes. Ready to serve: 1 hour.

Per serving: 250 calories, 7 g total fat (1.5 g saturated fat), 16.5 mg cholesterol, 1495 mg sodium, 8 g fiber.

GRILLED POLENTA

COOKING TECHNIQUE: DIRECT, HIGH HEAT

Some people say polenta is just cornmeal mush. But those in the know see it as an Italian delicacy — especially when you spice it up and grill it. Serve this easy side with any roasted meat or bird.

3½ cups milk (whole or low-fat)

¼ teaspoon salt

1½ cups cornmeal

1 tablespoon minced fresh rosemary

1 tablespoon minced fresh parsley

½ cup freshly grated Parmesan cheese

¼ cup olive oil

1 Butter 11x7-inch baking pan. In large saucepan, bring milk and salt to a simmer over medium heat. Sprinkle in cornmeal, stirring constantly with wooden spoon until smooth; reduce heat to low. Cook 20 minutes, stirring constantly. Mix in rosemary, parsley and Parmesan; immediately spread into pan. Cool to room temperature. Cover; refrigerate until firm, at least 2 hours or up to 3 days.

2 Heat grill for direct cooking.

3 Turn pan upside down to remove polenta in 1 piece. Cut into 12 squares or triangles. Brush both sides of cut pieces with olive oil.

4 Place polenta slices on gas grill directly over high heat or on charcoal grill 4 to 6 inches directly over high-heat coals. Cover; grill, turning once, 8 minutes or until lightly browned.

6 servings.

Preparation time: 1 hour, 10 minutes. Ready to serve: 3 hours, 10 minutes.

Per serving: 325 calories, 15.5 g total fat (5 g saturated fat), 20 mg cholesterol, 330 mg sodium, 2.5 g fiber.

GRILLED ANTIPASTI WITH NO-FUSS AIOLI

Kick off your next barbecue with a plate of antipasti, those marinated vegetables so popular in Italian cooking. Aioli is an uncooked garlic sauce made with oil and eggs — but here made with mayonnaise for simplicity.

AIOLI

1½ cups mayonnaise

3   garlic cloves or to taste, crushed

1   tablespoon lemon juice

1   tablespoon Dijon mustard

1   teaspoon salt

½   teaspoon freshly ground pepper

VEGETABLES

1   medium red onion, sliced into ½-inch-thick rings

1   medium fennel bulb, trimmed, cut into ¼-inch-thick slices

1   lb. asparagus spears, trimmed

2   red bell peppers, cut into 1-inch-thick strips

2   (6-oz.) zucchini, cut lengthwise into long ¼-inch-long slices

12   canned artichoke bottoms

1   (8-oz.) bottle Italian dressing

8   sprigs rosemary, soaked in water 30 minutes, then drained

1   **For Aioli:** In medium bowl, mix mayonnaise, garlic, lemon juice, Dijon, salt and pepper until smooth. Cover; refrigerate until ready to serve. Aioli can be prepared ahead. Store, covered, in refrigerator up to 5 days.

2   **For Vegetables:** Place red onion, fennel, asparagus, bell peppers, zucchini and artichokes in large bowl or roasting pan; pour bottled dressing over. Turn to coat; marinate at room temperature 30 minutes, tossing frequently.

3   Heat grill for direct cooking. If using gas grill, place rosemary sprigs directly on lava rocks; if using charcoal grill, place directly on high-heat coals.

4   Place red onion and fennel directly over high heat. Cover; grill, turning once, 8 minutes or until golden and soft. Transfer to serving platter.

5   Place asparagus and bell peppers directly over high heat. Cover; grill, turning once, 5 minutes or until browned. Transfer to serving platter.

6   Place zucchini and artichokes directly over high heat. Cover; grill, turning once, 4 minutes or until browned. Transfer to serving platter. Serve with reserved Aioli.

8 servings.

Preparation time: 20 minutes. Ready to serve: 1 hour, 10 minutes.

Per serving: 380 calories, 36 g total fat (5.5 g saturated fat), 25 mg cholesterol, 715 mg sodium, 4 g fiber.

Smoky Southwest Skillet Cornbread, page 156

BREADS

Bread comes off a grill grate baked just right. Frankly, the grill is a perfect oven for bread, which needs high, radiant heat to form a good crust and dense inner structure. Some grill breads bake on indirect heat while others are grilled over direct heat, especially if you have a gas grill with different heating ranks or zones. You can even bake some breads over direct heat while other meats barbecue at indirect heat. Give these "grilled" breads a try!

GARLIC BREAD

Everyone knows how terrific Garlic Bread *is. But with roasted garlic, right off the grill, it's even better.*

1 medium head garlic, outer papery husks removed

2 teaspoons olive oil

6 tablespoons unsalted butter, at room temperature

¼ cup freshly grated Parmesan cheese

¼ teaspoon salt

1 (20- to 22-inch) large loaf Italian bread or French baguette, cut in half lengthwise

1 Arrange grill for indirect cooking. Heat grill.

2 Meanwhile, cut top quarter off garlic head so all cloves are exposed; discard top. Place garlic head on small sheet of aluminum foil; drizzle olive oil over exposed cloves. Seal foil loosely around head.

3 Place foil packet on gas grill indirectly over medium heat or on charcoal grill to the side of medium-hot coals. Cover; cook about 40 minutes or until garlic is soft. Transfer to carving board; cool to room temperature without unwrapping.

4 If using gas grill, increase heat to high. If using charcoal grill, add more briquettes and allow fire to come to high heat.

5 Squeeze cooled garlic cloves from head into large bowl; add butter, Parmesan and salt. Mash with fork until uniform. Spread onto cut side of bread halves; put halves back together as original loaf. Wrap in aluminum foil. Place on gas or charcoal grill directly over high heat. Cover; cook 5 minutes or until butter melts.

6 Open foil; place bread directly over heat cut-side up to toast, about 1 minute or until browned, turning once.

10 to 12 servings.

Preparation time: 5 minutes. Ready to serve: 1 hour, 15 minutes.

Per serving: 270 calories, 11 g total fat (5.5 g saturated fat), 20 mg cholesterol, 505 mg sodium, 2 g fiber.

POPOVERS

You'll need a heavy-duty (preferably nonstick) popover pan to make these airy and light treats, great with rib roasts or elk loins. For a traditional British treat, omit the oil and use rendered beef fat, gathered from the drip pan underneath a rib roast.

3   eggs, at room
     temperature
1   cup milk (whole or
     low-fat)
2   tablespoons vegetable
     oil, plus additional for
     popover tins
½   teaspoon salt
1¼ cups all-purpose flour
6   popover tins

1 Heat grill for direct cooking.

2 In blender or food processor, combine eggs, milk, oil and salt; pulse twice to mix. Add flour; process 30 seconds or until smooth, scraping down sides of bowl as necessary.

3 Place popover tins on gas grill directly over high heat or on charcoal grill 4 to 6 inches directly over high-heat coals; cover. Heat 5 minutes. Oil popover tins. (Be careful: They're very hot; use barbecue oiling brush or many paper towels and wear grilling gloves.) Move tins to indirect heat or cooler part of grill rack. Divide batter among tins. Cover; bake 35 to 40 minutes or until golden.*

6 servings.

Preparation time: 10 minutes. Ready to serve: 1 hour.

Per serving: 190 calories, 8 g total fat (2 g saturated fat), 110 mg cholesterol, 245 mg sodium, 0.5 g fiber.

TIP *Resist opening the grill lid, especially during first 20 minutes of baking. Even the slightest breeze can cause these light popovers to collapse into a doughy mess. If you must check after the first 20 minutes, open the lid only an inch or so.

PIZZA ON THE GRILL

Pizza is a natural for the grill: fun and satisfying every time.

1 (¼-oz.) pkg. active dry yeast

6 tablespoons lukewarm water (105°F to 115°F)

2 tablespoons sweet, red-label vermouth

2 tablespoons olive oil, plus additional for bowl and grill grate

½ teaspoon salt

1½ to 2 cups all-purpose flour, plus additional for dusting work surface and dough

¾ cup bottled pizza sauce

1½ cups (6 oz.) shredded mozzarella cheese

1 tablespoon dried oregano

1 teaspoon crushed red pepper

1 In large bowl, stir yeast, lukewarm water and vermouth until dissolved; set aside to proof 5 minutes or until bubbly. With wooden spoon, stir in 2 tablespoons olive oil, salt and 1½ cups of the flour until smooth.

2 Turn dough onto lightly floured work surface. Knead 8 minutes by pulling dough with one hand while pressing into it with heel of other hand, adding flour in 2-tablespoon increments as necessary to create smooth dough. Alternately, place dough in stand mixer fitted with dough hook; knead 5 minutes at medium speed, adding flour in 2-tablespoon increments to create smooth dough.

3 Lightly oil large bowl. Add dough; turn to coat. Cover; place in warm dry place about 1 hour or until doubled in bulk.

4 Heat grill for direct cooking. Flour 1 side of dough. Place floured-side down in 16-inch pizza pan or baking sheet; press in circle to fit pan or create 16-inch circle on baking sheet. Top with pizza sauce, mozzarella, oregano and crushed red pepper. Add or substitute other toppings as you please.

5 Place pizza pan on gas grill directly over medium heat or on charcoal grill 4 to 6 inches directly over medium-hot coals. Cover; grill 15 minutes or until dough is firm and cheese melts.

6 When dough is firm, carefully slip pizza off pan or baking sheet onto grill grate directly over medium heat or medium-hot coals. Grill 1 minute or until bottom is lightly charred.

4 servings.

Preparation time: 10 minutes. Ready to serve: 1 hour, 40 minutes.

Per serving: 390 calories, 16.5 g total fat (6 g saturated fat), 20 mg cholesterol, 725 mg sodium, 2.5 g fiber.

NA'AN

This Indian bread is often served with dishes like Tandoori Chicken *(page 77), but would be equally at home with* Stuffed Bell Peppers *(page 139) or* Lamb Shish Kabobs *(page 91). Although traditionally made in a fiery tandoor oven, Na'an works almost as well on the grill. The bread puffs slightly, creating a light and airy pocket.*

1	(¼-oz.) pkg. active dry yeast
1	tablespoon sugar
1¼	cups warm water (105°F to 115°F)
1	egg, lightly beaten
2	tablespoons vegetable oil, plus more for bowl, platter and grill grate
2	tablespoons honey
2	teaspoons salt
4 to 5	cups all-purpose flour, plus additional for dusting work surface
¼	cup (½ stick) unsalted butter, melted, cooled

1 In large bowl, stir yeast and sugar in warm water until dissolved; let sit 5 minutes to proof, until bubbly. Stir in egg, oil, honey and salt until well combined. Add 3 cups of the flour; mix with wooden spoon until smooth. Add flour in ½-cup increments, mixing with your hands until smooth dough is formed.

2 Turn out onto lightly floured work surface. Knead 4 minutes by hand, pulling with one hand while pressing into dough with heel of other hand, adding flour in 1-tablespoon increments as necessary to create smooth, nonsticky dough.

3 Lightly oil large bowl; place dough inside, then turn to coat. Cover; set aside in warm, dry, place about 1½ hours or until doubled in bulk.

4 Heat grill for direct cooking. Punch dough down; divide into 12 equal balls. Place on oiled platter; cover loosely. Set in warm, dry place about 30 minutes or until puffy.

5 Brush grill grate with oil. Lightly flour hands. Take 1 dough ball; flatten between palms of yours hands, stretching it to 8-inch oval.* Place on gas grill directly over medium heat or on charcoal grill 4 to 6 inches directly over medium-hot coals. Cover; grill, turning once, 5 to 6 minutes or until puffed. Brush 1 side with melted butter before serving.

6 servings.

Preparation time: 1 hour, 10 minutes. Ready to serve: 3 hours, 10 minutes.

Per serving: 455 calories, 14 g total fat (6 g saturated fat), 55 mg cholesterol, 840 mg sodium, 2.5 g fiber.

TIP *Traditionally, Na'an is shaped like a teardrop. But there's no need to be fussy about it — the bread will come out fine in any shape. Yet authenticity sometimes counts, depending on your guests.

SMOKY SOUTHWEST SKILLET CORNBREAD

COOKING TECHNIQUE: DIRECT, HIGH HEAT, THEN INDIRECT, MEDIUM HEAT

You'll need a 12-inch cast-iron skillet to make cornbread on the grill. The cast iron takes the high heat and makes a delicious crust on the bread. We've added grilled vegetables to make the cornbread even smokier. If you like a sweeter cornbread, add 2 teaspoons sugar to the batter.

1   ear corn, husked, silks removed
1   poblano chile
1½ cups cornmeal
½   cup all-purpose flour
4   teaspoons baking powder
½   teaspoon salt
1¼ cups buttermilk
¼   cup vegetable oil, plus additional for skillet
2   eggs, at room temperature

1 Heat grill for direct cooking.

2 Place corn and poblano on gas grill directly over high heat or on charcoal grill 4 to 6 inches directly over high-heat coals. Cover; grill, turning frequently, 8 minutes or until corn is browned and poblano is charred.

3 Transfer corn to carving board; let stand 5 minutes. Place poblano in small bowl; cover tightly with plastic wrap. Steam 10 minutes.

4 Slice kernels off cob; place in large bowl. Discard cob. Peel poblano. Core, seed and chop; place in bowl with corn. Stir in cornmeal, flour, baking powder and salt. In medium bowl, whisk buttermilk, oil and eggs until uniform. Pour into dry ingredients; mix with wooden spoon just until combined.

5 Arrange grill for indirect cooking. If using gas grill, reduce heat to medium. If using charcoal grill, close vents to reduce heat to medium.

6 Oil 12-inch cast-iron skillet; pour in batter. Place on gas grill indirectly over medium heat or on charcoal grill indirectly to the side of medium-hot coals. Cover; bake 30 to 40 minutes or until browned and set.

8 servings.

Preparation time: 30 minutes. Ready to serve: 1 hour, 10 minutes.

Per serving: 203 calories, 9.5 g total fat (2 g saturated fat), 55 mg cholesterol, 440 mg sodium, 2.5 g fiber.

Grilled Pears, Tuscan Style, page 166

DESSERTS

When you take the meat off the grate, don't turn off the gas or put out the embers. Dessert is yet to come, and it doesn't have to be some indoor fandango! No, you can't make pastry cream on the grill. But who wants to fuss with a complicated dessert at the end of a grilling party? Whether you want to do something fun, elegant ... or maybe a little of both ... these ideas will inspire you.

NEW S'MORES

COOKING TECHNIQUE: DIRECT, HIGH HEAT

Use the coals remaining from your barbecue dinner to toast the marshmallows for this camp favorite. One warning: A barbecue grill is big and very hot. This dessert isn't kid-friendly — you'll need to make it for them. But the kids just might have to wrestle these s'mores away from the adults! Double or triple this recipe at will.

8	whole graham crackers
1	(4-oz.) thin white chocolate bar, cut into 4 pieces
12	large marshmallows
¼	cup chopped macadamia nuts
1	(4-oz.) thin dark chocolate bar, cut into 4 pieces

1 Remove grill grate. Heat grill for direct cooking.

2 Lay 4 graham crackers round-side down on work surface. Top each with 1 piece white chocolate.

3 Push marshmallows on ends of each skewer or wooden stick. If using skewers, wear grilling gloves or use heavy-duty hot pads. Toast marshmallows over low heat or low-heat coals about 3 minutes or until browned.

4 Using fork to remove hot marshmallows from skewers, place 3 on top of each white chocolate piece. Sprinkle hot marshmallows with 1 tablespoon nuts. Top each with 1 piece dark chocolate, then graham cracker, pressing gently to create sandwich. Allow marshmallows' heat to soften chocolate, about 1 minute. Other topping ideas include: almond or cashew butter, apple or pear butter, jam, jarred caramel sauce, jelly, marmalade, nutella, peanut butter, and preserves.

4 servings.

Preparation time: 15 minutes. Ready to serve: 20 minutes.

Per serving: 515 calories, 25 g total fat (11.5 g saturated fat), 5 mg cholesterol, 195 mg sodium, 2.5 g fiber.

GRILLED PEACH BANANA SPLITS

Move over Dairy Queen — here's true summer delight. The peaches and bananas are grilled, just until soft and golden. Make sure ice cream is at the ready, so it goes into the bowl with the warm fruit and begins to melt right into the sauces.

4   barely-ripe freestone peaches, peeled, halved and pitted

¼   cup (½ stick) unsalted butter, melted

2   teaspoons packed light brown sugar

4   large ripe bananas

4   scoops vanilla ice cream

4   scoops chocolate ice cream

4   scoops strawberry ice cream

1   cup purchased pineapple topping

1   cup purchased caramel topping

1   cup purchased chocolate topping

1 Heat grill for direct cooking.

2 Place peaches cut-side down on gas grill directly over medium heat or on charcoal grill 4 to 6 inches directly over medium-hot coals. Brush with melted butter. Cover; grill 3 minutes. Turn with metal spatula; brush with melted butter. Sprinkle each with ¼ teaspoon brown sugar. Peel bananas; place on grill directly over medium heat; brush with melted butter. Cover; grill, turning bananas once, 3 minutes or until sugar melts on peaches and bananas are lightly browned. Transfer to carving board. Slice peach halves in half; slice bananas in half lengthwise.

3 Place 2 banana slices along sides of each banana split dish or bowl. Place 4 peach quarters in each bowl. Add 1 scoop each of vanilla, chocolate and strawberry ice cream to each

bowl. Top with ¼ cup each pineapple, caramel and chocolate toppings.

4 Other toppings include: cherries, chocolate sprinkles, chopped dried figs, chopped pecans or walnuts, colored sugar, miniature marshmallows, raisins or currants, sliced almonds, toasted shredded sweetened coconut, and whipped cream.

4 servings.

Preparation time: 20 minutes. Ready to serve: 30 minutes.

Per serving: 1090 calories, 38 g total fat (21 g saturated fat), 95 mg cholesterol, 505 mg sodium, 6.5 g fiber.

BAKED APPLES ON THE GRILL

Baked apples have long been a winter favorite. Now they are for summer too! They're easy and quick, right off the grill. Buy apples meant for baking, like Granny Smiths — others will break down and become mush as the filling melts, and applesauce simply is not a grilled food!

4   (9-oz.) firm tart baking apples

½   cup chopped pecans

¼   cup (½ stick) unsalted butter, melted, cooled

¼   cup currants or raisins, chopped

3   tablespoons packed dark brown sugar

½   teaspoon salt

½   teaspoon ground cinnamon

¼   teaspoon grated nutmeg

Vegetable oil for grill grate

1 Heat grill for direct cooking.

2 Core apples by placing them stem-side down on work surface; scoop out seeds. Core with melon baller or grapefruit spoon beginning at end that's now facing up. Leave as much flesh as possible; do not break skin or break through stem end.

3 In medium bowl, mix pecans, butter, currants, brown sugar, salt, cinnamon and nutmeg until uniform. Pack filling into apples where cored.

4 Brush grill grate with oil. Place apples stuffing-side up on gas grill directly over medium heat or on charcoal grill directly over medium-hot coals. Cover; grill about 20 minutes or until apples are tender and slightly saggy and filling is bubbly. Transfer to carving board; let stand 5 minutes before serving.

4 servings.

Preparation time: 30 minutes. Ready to serve: 50 minutes.

Per serving: 350 calories, 22 g total fat (8 g saturated fat), 30 mg cholesterol, 295 mg sodium, 5.5 g fiber.

GRILLED FIGS

Figs always make a simple summer dessert — and are somehow even better when grilled. Buy fresh figs that are hardly ripe, not soft. They'll soften on the grill after only a few minutes, and become even sweeter. Taking soft, ripe figs off the grill when they're stacked close together can be challenging (so see the tip below).

½ cup crème fraîche or sour cream

½ teaspoon vanilla

½ teaspoon sugar
Vegetable oil for grill grate

8 large barely ripened fresh figs, halved*

¼ cup (½ stick) unsalted butter, cut into 16 pieces (or each tablespoon cut into fourths), at room temperature

½ teaspoon grated nutmeg

½ cup maple syrup, warmed

1 Heat grill for direct cooking.

2 In small bowl, stir crème fraîche, vanilla and sugar until sugar dissolves.

3 Brush grill grate with oil. Place figs cut-side up on gas grill directly over medium heat or on charcoal grill 4 to 6 inches directly over medium-hot coals. Dot each fig half with 1 piece (¼ tablespoon) butter; sprinkle each with dash nutmeg. Cover; grill about 2 minutes or just until butter melts and figs soften.

4 Meanwhile, place 2 tablespoons crème fraîche mixture in center of each of 4 plates. Gently remove figs from grill with metal spatula. Place 4 fig halves on each plate, nesting them in créme fraiche. Drizzle 2 tablespoons warm maple syrup over each plate to serve.

4 servings.

Preparation time: 30 minutes. Ready to serve: 35 minutes.

Per serving: 360 calories, 17.5 g total fat (11 g saturated fat), 50 mg cholesterol, 15 mg sodium, 4 g fiber.

TIP *Because figs are soft and have a high sugar content, they stick and can make a mess unless the grate is well oiled. Use a natural bristle pastry brush or saturated paper towel. For extra protection, you can also oil the skins of the figs before you slice them. When oiling the grill, always use a barbecue glove to protect your hand from the grill's heat.

GRILLED PEARS, TUSCAN STYLE

Popular in Tuscany, this simple dessert is often served after a grilled meal — or even as a midafternoon pick-me-up with an espresso. Choose a strong-flavored honey such as pine tree, lavender, buckwheat or oak to match the sliced Parmesan. If you were ever going to spring for a wedge of aged Parmesan, now is the time.

4	firm ripe pears
3	tablespoons almond oil or walnut oil
1	teaspoon sugar
4	oz. Parmesan cheese, cut into thin slices*
2	tablespoons plus 2 teaspoons honey, preferably dark

1 Heat grill for direct cooking.

2 Slice pears into ½-inch-thick slices. Core slices as necessary, removing seeds. Place in large bowl; toss with oil and sugar to coat.

3 Place pear slices on gas grill directly over high heat or on charcoal grill over high-heat coals. Cover; grill 6 minutes, turning once. Transfer pears to dessert plates; top with Parmesan. Let rest 5 minutes as cheese softens from pears' warmth. Drizzle each plate with 2 teaspoons honey.

4 servings.

Preparation time: 20 minutes. Ready to serve: 30 minutes.

Per serving: 365 calories, 19.5 g total fat (6 g saturated fat), 20 mg cholesterol, 530 mg sodium, 4 g fiber.

TIP *A cheese plane works best for cutting thin cheese slices.

RECICE INDEX

This index lists every recipe in Grill Thrills! *by name. If you're looking for a specific recipe but can't recall the exact name, turn to the General Index that starts on page 169.*

GENERAL INDEX

There are several ways to use this helpful index. First — you can find recipes by name. Second — if you don't know a recipe's specific name but recall a feature or special ingredient, look under that heading and all the related recipes will be listed; scan for the recipe you want. Finally — you can use this general index to find a summary of recipes in each chapter of the book (beef, poultry, vegetables, etc.).

A

Apples
Baked Apples on the Grill, 163
Pork Chops Stuffed with Grilled Apple Chutney, 51
Apricot Grilled Pheasant with a Grilled Apricot Relish, 102–103
Artichoke
Grilled Antipasti with No-fuss Aioli, 146
Asparagus
Grilled Antipasti with No-fuss Aioli, 146
Stuffed Flank Steak with a Hoisin Marinade, 46–47
Avocados
Fajitas in a Sangria Marinade, 41

B

Baked Apples on the Grill, 163
Baked Beans, 144
Bananas
Grilled Peach Banana Splits, 162
Barbecued Whole Turkey with a Cajun Rub, 71
Barbecued Wild Duck with a Chunky Sour Cherry Sauce, 105
Barbecue sauce
Basic Grilled Chicken with a Sweet and Spicy Barbecue Sauce, 75
Beef Ribs with a Plum Barbecue Sauce, 38
Bourbon Baby Back Ribs with a Maple Barbecue Sauce, 59
Chinese Spare Ribs, 57

Swordfish Kabobs with a Walnut Paprika Barbecue Sauce, 127
Texas Brisket with Classic Texas Barbecue Sauce, 34–35
Barbecuing
defined, 8
Basic Grilled Chicken with a Sweet and Spicy Barbecue Sauce, 75
Baskets, grilling, 22
Beans
Baked Beans, 144
Beef, 27–48
Beef Ribs with a Plum Barbecue Sauce, 38
Beef Tenderloin, 30
Chili on the Grill, 36
doneness temperatures, 18
Fajitas in a Sangria Marinade, 41
Inside-Out Cheeseburgers, 43
London Broil, 42
Midwestern Hamburgers, 39
Rib Eye Steaks with a Mole Rub, 31
Rib Roast with Grilled Pineapple Poblano Salsa, 32–33
Strip Steaks with Rosemary Honey Butter, 28
Stuffed Flank Steak with a Hoisin Marinade, 46–47
Texas Brisket with Classic Texas Barbecue Sauce, 34–35
Vietnamese Grilled Beef Salad, 44
Beef Ribs with a Plum Barbecue Sauce, 38
Beef Tenderloin, 30

Bourbon Baby Back Ribs with a Maple Barbecue Sauce, 59
Breads, 149–156
Garlic Bread, 150
Na'an, 154
Pizza on the Grill, 153
Popovers, 151
Smoky Southwest Skillet Cornbread, 156
Brush, grill, 20
Buffalo Chicken Wings with a Blue Cheese Dip, 74
Butcher twine, 19
Butters. *See* Sauces and butters

C

Carving board with trough, 23
Charcoal chimney, 16
Charcoal grills
cleaning, 24
cooking over indirect heat, 17
defined, 9
evaluating, 12
lighting fire, 15–16
maintaining fire, 16
oiling grill grate, 25
pros/cons of, 13
temperature notes, 17
wood chips on, 17
Cherries
Barbecued Wild Duck with a Chunky Sour Cherry Sauce, 105
Chicken. *See* Poultry
Chicken Sitting on a Beer Can, 78
Chili on the Grill, 36
Chinese Spare Ribs, 57
Cider-Marinated Venison Loin, 101
Coconut-Rubbed Pork Satay, 65

169

RECIPES AND NOTES

RECIPES AND NOTES

RECIPES AND NOTES